CORNERSMITH

When Alex Elliott-Howery and James Grant opened the doors to Cornersmith, their neighbourhood cafe on an unassuming street corner in Sydney's inner west, they wanted the food to represent the sustainable ethos they held to when cooking at home: making everything from scratch using local, in-season produce; avoiding processed foods; and pickling and preserving to reduce waste. But most importantly, they wanted to serve great-tasting, good-for-you food that everyone would love.

From day one the locals flocked in, and Cornersmith has since grown to incorporate a picklery, cooking school and trading system where customers can swap home-grown produce for a coffee or a jar of pickles.

This book brings together favourite dishes from the award-winning cafe, covering everything from breakfasts, lunches and dinners to desserts, as well as recipes for their most popular pickles, jams, compotes, chutneys, relishes and fermented foods. Cornersmith food is about following the seasons, not the latest fad; it's about opening your eyes to the bounty available in your own neighbourhood and showing you how best to use it.

CORNERSMITH

Recipes from the cafe and picklery

Alex Elliott-Howery and James Grant

MURDOCH BOOKS

CONTENTS

About us	6
Spring	12
Summer	70
Autumn	122
Winter	190
Preserving	246
Recipe basics	260
About Cornersmith	262
Index	266
Acknowledgements	271

ABOUT US

We first started thinking about opening a cafe when our kids were really little. Probably having the same fantasies a lot of people do, about working for yourself and creating the kind of local place you wish was on your street.

James had been working in cafes, bars and with coffee roasters for years, and felt like he was ready to open his own place. At the time Alex was home with the kids and turning family meals into creative projects: researching food ethics and eating seasonally, making everything from scratch and discovering an obsessive love for pickling. We felt that somehow we could put our skills and knowledge together and make a family business that would contribute something to the community.

After endless conversations about it, we decided to take the plunge. We knew from the beginning that if we were going to open a cafe, we needed to apply the same sustainable philosophy we lived by at home and make it work in a business setting. It was from this principle that all our plans were made. And with the helping hands of friends and family we gutted an old run-down corner shop close to our home and turned it into our cafe. Cornersmith opened its doors in January 2012, and the party was quite something. We papered the windows, roasted a goat on the spit in the backyard and danced on the tables until the early hours of the morning.

Soon after, in our very first week of business, we faced a setback. One night, after we'd locked up and gone home for the day, the windows were smashed in and aggressive graffiti was scrawled all over the shop. We were so sad, but what followed was an outpouring of community support. As we were cleaning up the wreckage, people came by with flowers, letters and hand-made cards to show how welcome we really were. Somebody even brought us a home-grown watermelon with a big bow on it!

From then on, Cornersmith has been full. The response has been incredible. Our focus on sustainability, seasonality, sourcing local produce from small-scale growers and makers, and reducing waste, has struck a chord with our community. When it all began, we had no idea that our vision would be appreciated and supported so positively, and we feel very privileged to be part of such a forward-thinking community.

Given the strength of this community spirit, once Cornersmith was up and running, we started to wonder how a trading system would be received. So we set up a way for our customers to bring in their excess backyard produce in exchange for coffee or pickles. It turned out that Marrickville gardeners were overloaded with citrus fruit, figs, chillies, basil and rosemary, and people started coming in every week to trade their home-grown bounty. The neighbourhood responded so well to the idea that soon Alex and her long-time pickling mate Jaimee were seeing boxes of mandarins and crates of chokos come through the door.

During that first year of business we kept the cafe closed on Mondays for bottling days, but we couldn't keep up with the demand for our preserves. Marrickville was hungry for pickles! We also had a lot of interest from people who wanted to learn how to make their own pickles and preserves. And so the picklery was born. Occupying an old butcher's shop on a corner up the hill from the cafe, this is where we do all our own bottling and run our food craft workshops: pickling, jam-making, fermenting, cheese-making, smoking, bread-making, pastry and more. It is the place where people come to trade, and to see what we are making that day. We also sell a range of carefully selected groceries from our suppliers.

All the recipes in this book are favourites from the cafe and picklery, not only because they are delicious, but because they reflect how we think and feel about food, community, and even business. Our menu brings together traded and small-scale farm produce, ethically raised meats, truly free-range eggs and slow food techniques. We are city folk through and through, running a business and raising a family, but that doesn't mean we don't have time to consider the source of our food and the impact of its consumption. We want to inspire people to make things at home, to think about where their food comes from, and to understand the seasonal availability of produce. If we can encourage people to connect with their communities and make considered choices in their homes and businesses, then we will feel like we have accomplished what we set out to do.

SPRING

PREPARATION TIME
15 minutes

COOKING TIME
about 1 hour

STORAGE
up to 12 months

MAKES
about 5 x 300 ml
(10½ fl oz) jars

STRAWBERRY, RHUBARB & ROSE JAM

There's not a lot of fruit around in early spring – pears and citrus fruit have finished up and there's still a few months to go before the stone fruits come in – so this is the time to make use of strawberries and rhubarb. This is a softer-set jam, to maintain a bright colour and flavour. It's delicious on buttered toast, of course, but is also great in cakes.

1 kg (2 lb 4 oz) strawberries, hulled and halved
1 kg (2 lb 4 oz) trimmed rhubarb stalks,
   cut into 2 cm (¾ in) pieces – about 2 bunches
1 kg (2 lb 4 oz) caster (superfine) sugar
juice and finely grated zest of 3 lemons
1½–2 teaspoons rosewater, to taste

Put the strawberries, rhubarb and 250 ml (9 fl oz/1 cup) of water into a jam pan or other wide, heavy-based pan. Bring to a simmer over low heat and cook until the fruit is soft and falling apart, about 20–30 minutes.

Remove from the heat and leave to cool for a minute or two, then stir in the sugar, lemon juice and zest.

Return to low heat and cook, stirring, until the sugar has completely dissolved. Turn up the heat and bring to the boil, then boil rapidly until setting point is reached (see page 251), stirring occasionally to prevent it sticking to the bottom of the pan. Keep in mind that as both these fruits are low in pectin, this jam will set like a soft conserve. Start to test for setting point after 20 minutes and then every 5 minutes after that – it could take as long as 40 minutes.

Meanwhile, sterilise your jars (see page 250).

Once you are happy with the set of your jam, turn off the heat and leave to cool for a minute or so, then stir in 1½ teaspoons of the rosewater. Taste to see if you need more. Remember a little rosewater goes a long way!

Carefully pour the hot jam into the hot jars, then seal immediately and store in a cool, dark place for up to 12 months.

CORNERSMITH TOASTED MUESLI

This is our chef Sabine's toasted muesli, and it's often on the breakfast menu at the cafe. The addition of tahini means it's nice and nutty, without being too sweet. It also makes the muesli cook to quite a rich dark brown, so don't be alarmed and think it's burning while you're toasting it. Depending on your oven, this might take longer than the time given. If you're not sure, just test one of the almonds to see if it's toasted right through – if it is, your muesli is ready.

This goes well with the rhubarb on page 58, or either of the compotes on pages 63 and 118. If you want to double the recipe, it keeps well in an airtight container for about 2 weeks. If you end up storing the muesli for longer than this and it gets a bit stale, just toast it in the oven again for 10–15 minutes at 140°C (275°F/gas mark 1).

PREPARATION TIME
10 minutes

COOKING TIME
1¼ hours

MAKES
about 300 g (10½ oz)

60 g (2¼ oz) honey
30 g (1 oz) tahini
2 teaspoons vegetable oil
20 g (¾ oz) brown sugar
100 g (3½ oz/1 cup) rolled (porridge) oats
25 g (1 oz) sunflower seeds
25 g (1 oz) linseeds
30 g (1 oz) almonds
10 g (¼ oz) poppy seeds
30 g (1 oz) puffed rice

Preheat the oven to 150°C (300°F/gas mark 2) and line a large baking tray with baking paper.

Combine the honey, tahini, vegetable oil, brown sugar and 30 ml (1 fl oz) water in a small saucepan. Cook over low heat, stirring, until the sugar and honey have dissolved and everything is combined.

Put all the remaining ingredients into a large bowl, then pour in the honey and tahini mixture. Combine thoroughly, so that all the dry ingredients are coated.

Spread out the muesli on the prepared baking tray and bake for approximately 45 minutes. It's very important to move the muesli around during the toasting process so it toasts evenly – do this at least once every 15 minutes. Reduce the oven temperature to 100°C (200°F/gas mark ½) and bake for another 15–20 minutes or until the muesli is dry and evenly toasted, again stirring the mix a few times as it cooks. Leave to cool before serving.

PREPARATION TIME
30 minutes

COOKING TIME
5 minutes

SERVES 4

SPRING GREEN SALAD

This is a light fresh salad, showcasing the best of springtime. For us, it is spring in a bowl. We use lots of chive flowers at this time of year. They're so pretty that it's tempting to cover the salad with them, but their flavour is very intense, so go easy.

200 g (7 oz) podded peas
200 g (7 oz) podded broad beans
juice and finely grated zest of 1 lemon, kept separate
4 baby artichokes or 1 large globe artichoke
4 asparagus spears
2 handfuls watercress, picked
pinch of chilli flakes – optional
50 ml (1¾ fl oz) olive oil
50 g (1¾ oz) fetta, finely crumbled
chive flowers, to garnish – optional

Bring a medium saucepan of water to the boil and blanch the peas for 1 minute, then refresh under cold running water and drain well. Bring the water back to the boil and blanch the broad beans for 2 minutes, then refresh and drain. Double-peel the broad beans by pressing them gently between your fingers; the bright-green beans should slip out of the greyish skins. Set aside.

Fill a bowl with water and add half of the lemon juice. If using baby artichokes, remove the stems and pull off the tough outer leaves. Once you reach the softer, paler leaves, use a sharp knife to cut off the top three-quarters of the artichokes, so you are left with just the bottom quarters – drop them into the bowl of lemon water as you go, to stop them discolouring. If using a large globe artichoke, use a sharp knife to remove the outer layers of the artichoke until the firm heart is exposed. Scrape out the hairy choke with a small teaspoon and slip the artichoke heart straight into the lemon water.

Drain the artichokes and pat dry with paper towel. Using a mandoline or very sharp knife, shave the artichokes into paper-thin slices. Transfer the slices to a large bowl and drizzle with the remaining lemon juice, tossing to coat well. Finely shave the asparagus lengthways using a mandoline or vegetable peeler. Add to the bowl, along with the peas, broad beans, lemon zest, watercress and chilli flakes, if using. Season with salt and pepper, then gently toss everything together and drizzle with the olive oil.

Serve topped with the crumbled fetta. If you have chive flowers, gently ease them apart and scatter the petals over the salad.

GREEN TOMATO & RICOTTA SALAD

PREPARATION TIME
10 minutes

SERVES
4 to accompany grilled meat or fish

Green tomatoes are one of the first signs of the warmer weather. Although they're just unripe red tomatoes, they're crisp, firm and sharp, almost like a different vegetable. Sadly, they don't get used much and it's unusual to see them in recipes. We love them, though, and so for us the end of spring is the time for green tomato salads, green tomato relish and pickled green cherry tomatoes.

This year we've been getting our green tomatoes from Omar in Hoxton Park, western Sydney. He's quite perplexed by the amount of green tomatoes we've been ordering, and he keeps telling us to wait until they turn red. If you're growing your own tomatoes, just pick them early. If not, try farmers' markets or speciality fruit and vegetable suppliers. Our local Lebanese grocers sell them by the boxful.

This light, refreshing salad is a great way to use raw green tomatoes. It's essential to use a mandoline or a sharp serrated knife in order to slice them thinly. If you don't have any ricotta, you could use fetta or some aged pecorino or parmesan instead.

6–8 green tomatoes, thinly sliced
1½ tablespoons apple balsamic vinegar,
   aged sherry vinegar or balsamic vinegar
½ teaspoon dijon mustard
100 ml (3½ fl oz) olive oil
small handful (¼ cup) mixed herbs, such as dill,
   oregano, tarragon, chives
chive flowers – optional
150 g (5½ oz) ricotta

Place the tomatoes in a large bowl. Sprinkle with a pinch of salt, toss gently and then set aside for 5 minutes to soften.

Meanwhile, make a vinaigrette by whisking the vinegar and mustard with a little salt and pepper, then slowly drizzling in the olive oil.

Add the vinaigrette to the tomatoes and gently toss to coat. Tear or chop the herbs, then add half to the tomatoes and mix through. Place the tomatoes on plates, scatter with the rest of the herbs and the chive flowers, if using, and top with small dollops of ricotta.

PREPARATION TIME
15 minutes

COOKING TIME
2¼ hours

SERVES 4

SPRING VEGETABLE CHICKEN SOUP

A clear, pretty soup that celebrates all the goodness of springtime: peas, asparagus, broad beans, herbs and baby carrots, with extra crunch and nuttiness from the sprouts (see page 261 for more on sprouting).

Roasting the chicken first gives the soup a deeper flavour and a golden colour – get your butcher to cut the chicken into quarters, and ask for some extra chicken bones to roast for even more flavour, if you like. The left-over chicken meat can be used on a bagel (see page 29) or sandwich, or tossed through the slaw on page 42. If you have any soup left over, freeze the clear, strained stock, minus the vegetables. Stock is always a good thing to have in the freezer.

175 g (6 oz/1 cup) podded broad beans
3 baby carrots, very thinly sliced
2 cm (¾ in) knob of ginger, cut into fine julienne strips
155 g (5½ oz/1 cup) podded peas
4 asparagus spears, thinly sliced
2 tablespoons finely chopped parsley
1 teaspoon finely chopped chives
60 g (2¼ oz/½ cup) mixed sprouts
   (see page 261) – optional

CHICKEN STOCK
1 x 1.6–2 kg (3 lb 8 oz–4 lb 8 oz) free-range chicken,
   cut into 4 pieces
5 thyme sprigs
3 bay leaves
handful parsley stalks
2 large onions, peeled and cut in half
2 small carrots, peeled and cut in half
4 celery stalks, cut into 5 cm (2 in) lengths
1 garlic bulb, cut in half crossways
5 allspice berries
3 cloves
15 black peppercorns

For the stock, preheat the oven to 180°C (350°F/gas mark 4) and line a roasting tin with baking paper.

Season the chicken pieces with salt, then place in the prepared tin and roast in the oven for 25–30 minutes or until golden brown. Discard the fat, then transfer the chicken to a large saucepan or stockpot, cover with cold water and add a couple of pinches of salt. Bring to a simmer over low heat, skimming off any froth from the surface. Tie the thyme, bay leaves and parsley stalks into a little bundle with string (so they'll be easier to remove later) and add to the stock, along with the onions, carrots, celery, garlic, allspice, cloves and peppercorns. If necessary, add more water to cover everything well, then bring to a gentle simmer and cook for about 1½ hours, skimming occasionally and adding more water as needed.

Lift the chicken pieces out of the stock and, when they are cool enough to handle, remove the meat from the bones. Tear one of the chicken breasts into small strips and set aside for the soup. Cover the rest of the meat with a little stock and keep for later use – it will keep in the fridge for up to 3 days.

Bring a small saucepan of water to the boil and blanch the broad beans for 2 minutes, then refresh under cold running water and drain. Double-peel the broad beans by pressing them gently between your fingers – the bright-green beans should slip out of the greyish skins.

Strain the stock into a clean pan, discarding the herbs, spices and vegetables. Place over low–medium heat, add the baby carrots and ginger and simmer for about 2–3 minutes. Next add the broad beans, peas and asparagus and simmer for 3–5 minutes until all the vegetables are just tender. Finally, add the chicken breast meat to gently warm through and adjust the seasoning, if needed.

Serve the soup straightaway in warmed soup bowls, garnished with the parsley, chives and sprouts, if using.

BAGEL WITH PULLED CHICKEN, MISO MAYONNAISE & GARLIC CHIPS

PREPARATION TIME
20 minutes

COOKING TIME
15 minutes

SERVES 4

This recipe is a great way to use up the meat from the chicken thighs after you've made the chicken soup on page 24. The garlic chips add a unique, sweet crunch. They may seem a bit fiddly, but they're an amazing thing to have in your repertoire. If you get a taste for them, make some extra, as they'll last for 3–4 days in an airtight container, and are great on salads or crumbled over buttered toast.

6 nice plump garlic cloves, thinly sliced using a mandoline or very sharp knife
500 ml (17 fl oz/2 cups) canola oil
1 teaspoon miso paste
1 quantity aioli (see page 97), made without the preserved lemon
2 cooked free-range chicken thighs (from making chicken stock – see page 24) or left-over roast chicken, meat taken off the bones and shredded
1 teaspoon chopped chives
1 teaspoon chopped chervil
splash of lemon or lime juice, if needed
4 seeded bagels, cut in half
60 g (2¼ oz/2 cups, lightly packed) watercress, picked
1 tablespoon chervil leaves

To make the garlic chips, combine the garlic slices and canola oil in a small saucepan. Place over medium heat and cook, stirring frequently, until the garlic is golden, about 15 minutes. Strain the garlic (reserving the garlic-infused oil for the next time) and drain on paper towel, spreading them out so they crisp as they cool. Season with salt.

Stir the miso paste into the aioli to make a miso mayonnaise. If the miso is very thick, loosen it with a teaspoon of water first, so it blends in more easily.

Combine the chicken, chives, chopped chervil and 1–2 tablespoons of the miso mayonnaise in a bowl, seasoning with salt and pepper. Taste and adjust as necessary – it may need sharpening with a little lemon or lime juice.

Lightly toast the bagel halves and spread with miso mayonnaise. Place the watercress and chervil leaves on the bottom half of each bagel, followed by the pulled chicken mixture. Top with the garlic chips and the other half of the bagel.

PREPARATION TIME
20 minutes, plus at least 2 hours resting (or overnight)

COOKING TIME
10 minutes

SERVES 4

ESCABECHE OF WHITING

Here's a traditional Mediterranean dish that is rather like a hot-pickled fish, as hot brine is poured over the fish fillets to 'preserve' them. If you can, leave it to sit overnight in the fridge to enhance the flavour, then warm it slightly and serve at room temperature. Eat this with crusty bread and aioli. You could substitute the whiting with red or grey mullet, sardines or other sustainable choices.

8 whiting fillets, skin on, pin-bones removed –
   ask your fishmonger to do this
70 ml (2¼ fl oz) olive oil
1 small carrot, thinly sliced
1 small fennel bulb, thinly sliced,
   any green fronds reserved
3 shallots, thinly sliced
2 garlic cloves, thinly sliced
1 unwaxed lemon, thinly sliced
2–3 thyme sprigs
2 bay leaves
1 teaspoon crushed coriander seeds
1 teaspoon crushed fennel seeds
100 ml (3½ fl oz) white wine vinegar
small handful (¼ cup) mixed torn fennel fronds,
   parsley, chervil and tarragon leaves
aioli (see page 97) and crusty bread, to serve

Season the fish fillets on both sides with salt and pepper. Heat 2 teaspoons of the olive oil in a large frying pan over medium–high heat and cook the fish, skin side down, for 1–2 minutes, then turn and cook for barely a minute on the other side. You want the flesh to still be slightly translucent, as the hot marinade will finish the cooking process. Transfer to a glass or ceramic dish that will hold the fillets in a single layer.

Pour the remaining 60 ml (2 fl oz/¼ cup) olive oil into a large pan over medium heat. Add the carrot, fennel, shallots and garlic and sweat until they start to soften, then add the lemon, thyme, bay leaves, coriander and fennel seeds, vinegar and 300 ml (10½ fl oz) water. Bring to the boil and season with salt and pepper, then reduce the heat and simmer for 5 minutes. Pour the hot marinade over the fish, then set aside to cool for 10–15 minutes, before transferring to the fridge for at least 2 hours or overnight.

To serve, bring the escabeche to room temperature, top with the fennel fronds and herbs and offer aioli on the side. Serve with crusty bread.

FENNEL, ORANGE & CHILLI SALT

We make lots of flavoured salts at Cornersmith, especially if we have an excess of herbs or citrus zest. This one is great to have on hand for seasoning barbecued or grilled white meats, fish (see page 93) and summer vegetables. Try other variations too, such as rosemary salt, thyme and sage salt, or a classic celery salt – just make sure whatever you're using is thoroughly dehydrated.

zest of 1 orange, peeled off in strips with a vegetable peeler
1½ teaspoons fennel seeds
200 g (7 oz) salt
¼ teaspoon chilli flakes

Preheat the oven to 140°C (275°F/gas mark 1).

Place the orange zest on a baking tray and dry in the oven for 15–20 minutes or until completely dried, then leave to cool. Grind to a fine powder using a spice grinder or pestle and mortar. Set aside.

Use a pestle and mortar to coarsely crush the fennel seeds, then transfer to a bowl. Add 1 teaspoon of the orange zest powder, the salt and the chilli flakes and mix to combine. Store in an airtight container.

PREPARATION TIME
10 minutes

COOKING TIME
20 minutes, plus 10 minutes cooling

STORAGE
up to 2 years

MAKES
about 200 g (7 oz)

PREPARATION TIME
10 minutes

COOKING TIME
45 minutes

SERVES
8 with drinks

SMOKY PAPRIKA & ROSEMARY TOASTED ALMONDS

These are absolutely delicious. We sell them in jars at the picklery and use them on our ploughman's plates. We also make them at home for every party and barbecue we have – they go down well with a beer. Watch out, though: these can be very addictive for young and old. Our daughter eats them by the jar!

If you're feeling adventurous, play with the spices and flavours: add chilli powder for more heat, or ground coriander or cumin with orange zest – you could even use the fennel, orange and chilli salt on page 33.

These almonds can be stored in an airtight container for up to 10 days, so it's worth doubling the recipe if you want to have a jar on hand.

2 teaspoons salt
1 teaspoon smoked paprika
50 ml (1¾ fl oz) olive oil
500 g (1 lb 2 oz) raw almonds
handful (⅓ cup) chopped rosemary

Preheat the oven to 140°C (275°F/gas mark 1) and line two baking trays with baking paper.

Combine the salt, smoked paprika and olive oil in a large bowl. Add the almonds and rosemary, then use your hands to mix everything together well.

Place the almonds on the prepared trays and spread them out evenly. Bake for 45 minutes or until the almonds are toasted through, shaking the trays every 10–15 minutes so they toast evenly.

Leave to cool to room temperature, then serve in bowls or small jars.

KRISTEN'S LABNEH

Cheese-maker Kristen Allan's labneh is a staple on our cafe menu. We serve it on our breakfast toast with fruit (see page 78) and in sandwiches. We also offer it at all our workshops – it's perfect with pickles and crackers to start a meal, or to serve at a party. Alternatively, labneh can be rolled into balls and marinated in olive oil: put the balls in a sterilised glass jar (see page 250), cover with olive oil and flavour with herbs, if you like. Stored in the fridge, it will keep for up to 3 months, as long as it's completely submerged in olive oil.

Kristen has very generously given us her recipe for this book. Her favourite way to serve labneh is thickly spread on a board, then scattered with nigella seeds and drizzled with good-quality olive oil.

For the best results, make your own yoghurt a few days beforehand or use a natural yoghurt with no additives – the only ingredients listed should be milk and cultures. A handy rule of thumb is that you'll need roughly double the amount of yoghurt compared to the amount of cheese you want to make.

Save the left-over whey to use in salad dressings (see page 260), or try our recipe for whey caramel (see page 238).

PREPARATION TIME
5 minutes, plus 24 hours draining

STORAGE
up to 2 weeks

MAKES
500 g (1 lb 2 oz)

1 kg (2 lb 4 oz) homemade or natural yoghurt
1 teaspoon fine sea salt

Line a colander with muslin (cheesecloth) and place a bowl underneath to catch the whey.

Mix the yoghurt with the salt and turn into the colander. Fold the corners of the muslin over to cover the yoghurt and place a small plate on top to press the cheese. Place in the fridge for 24 hours. Keep in mind that quite a bit of whey is going to come out, so you may need to drain off the whey every few hours.

The labneh should keep for up to 2 weeks in the fridge in a plastic container.

MEATBALLS, BROAD BEANS & YOGHURT

Meatballs are a hearty, wintry dish – but with a light tomato sauce, broad beans and yoghurt, they make a great springtime meal. You can substitute the lamb with pork or veal, or a mix of both.

PREPARATION TIME
20 minutes, plus 30 minutes chilling

COOKING TIME
1 hour

SERVES 4–6
(makes 24 meatballs)

- ¼ teaspoon allspice berries
- ½ teaspoon fennel seeds
- ¼ teaspoon coriander seeds
- ¼ teaspoon cumin seeds
- 2 teaspoons olive oil
- 1 onion, finely chopped
- 2 garlic cloves, crushed
- 500 g (1 lb 2 oz) minced (ground) lamb
- 1 free-range egg
- 1 tablespoon chopped parsley
- 1 teaspoon finely chopped preserved lemon rind
- pinch of cayenne pepper
- 90 g (3¼ oz/½ cup) broad beans, blanched and double-peeled (see page 18)
- 130 g (4½ oz/½ cup) natural yoghurt
- handful (½ cup, firmly packed) herb leaves, such as mint, dill and coriander, torn, to serve

TOMATO SAUCE
- 1 tablespoon olive oil
- 1 shallot, finely chopped
- 1 garlic clove, crushed
- 400 ml (14 fl oz) bottled tomatoes (see page 105) or 1 x 400 g (14 oz) tin tomatoes
- 1 bay leaf
- 2–3 sprigs of thyme
- 1 teaspoon finely chopped preserved lemon rind
- 100 ml (3½ fl oz) vermouth
- 200 ml (7 fl oz) chicken stock
- 1 tablespoon dried currants

Using a spice grinder or pestle and mortar, grind the allspice, fennel seeds, coriander seeds and cumin seeds to a fine powder. Heat 1 teaspoon of the olive oil in a frying pan over medium heat. Add the onion and garlic and cook for 5–8 minutes or until soft. Add the ground spices and cook for another 2–3 minutes, then remove from the heat and leave to cool slightly.

In a bowl, combine the cooled onion mixture with the lamb, egg, parsley and preserved lemon. Season with salt, pepper and the cayenne pepper. Use your hands to mix everything together well, then shape tablespoonfuls of the mixture into meatballs. Chill in the fridge for 30 minutes to firm them up.

For the tomato sauce, heat the olive oil in a heavy-based saucepan or flameproof casserole over medium heat. Add the shallot and garlic and sweat until soft, about 3–5 minutes. Add the tomatoes, bay leaf, thyme and preserved lemon, season with salt and pepper and simmer for 5 minutes. Finally, add the vermouth, stock and currants and simmer for another 10–15 minutes.

Meanwhile, heat ½ teaspoon of olive oil in a large frying pan over medium–high heat. Add some of the meatballs, being careful not to crowd the pan, and fry for a few minutes on each side until they are browned all over. Remove from the pan and set aside. Wipe out the pan and cook the rest of the meatballs the same way, using the remaining olive oil as needed.

Transfer the meatballs to the sauce and cover with a circle of baking paper, pressing it onto the surface. Cover with a lid and simmer for 20 minutes or until the meatballs are cooked through. Add the broad beans for the last 5 minutes, just to heat through. Drizzle with yoghurt and scatter over the herbs, then serve.

PREPARATION TIME
15 minutes

SERVES 4

KOHLRABI, CABBAGE & SPRING HERB SLAW WITH PICKLED CUMQUATS

One of our favourite Cornersmith slaws, this uses three vegetables from the Brassica family, all with different flavours and textures. Kohlrabi is very underrated, but is really worth looking for at the market or local greengrocer. Slightly sweeter than other members of the cabbage family, it can be eaten raw or cooked – try it out on your kids if they like raw carrots.

This slaw is perfect for your first spring barbecue. If you don't have a jar of pickled cumquats in your pantry, substitute fresh orange or blood orange segments and use their juice combined with some lemon juice in the dressing. And if you have some left-over shredded chicken breast in your fridge from making the soup on page 24, you could mix it through to make the slaw more substantial.

1 green or purple kohlrabi, peeled
150 g (5½ oz) savoy cabbage
4–6 cavolo nero leaves
4–6 pickled cumquats (see page 234), finely chopped
2 tablespoons chopped chives
large handful (½ cup, firmly packed) picked chervil
60 g (2¼ oz/½ cup) mixed sprouts (see page 261)

DRESSING
3 tablespoons liquid from pickled cumquats or other pickles
1 teaspoon dijon mustard
100 ml (3½ fl oz) olive oil

To make the dressing, combine the cumquat pickling liquid and mustard in a screw-top jar and season with salt and pepper. Add the olive oil, put the lid on and shake well to combine, then set aside.

Thinly slice the kohlrabi on a mandoline, then cut the slices into 5 mm (¼ in) wide strips. Shave the cabbage on the mandoline as well, then use a sharp knife to finely shred the cavolo nero.

In a large bowl, combine the kohlrabi with the savoy cabbage and cavolo nero. Add the chopped cumquats and three-quarters of the herbs. Pour over the dressing and very gently toss the salad, adjusting the seasoning with salt and pepper if necessary.

Serve the salad on a platter, garnished with sprouts and the remaining herbs.

PICKLED GREEN CHILLIES

These chillies are amazing – and funnily enough, they were a bit of a fluke. We found ourselves with a few extra boxes of chillies on our hands one week, so we poured a brine over them, popped them in the cool room, and proceeded to forget all about them. Six months later, we found them hiding on a high shelf and were blown away by their deliciousness!

These days they're a much-loved fixture on the menu at Cornersmith: they're great on their own, in a Mexican-style salsa or a potato salad (see page 146), or thinly sliced and tossed through raw salads and slaws to give them an extra kick. Try making these pickles with red chillies too.

PREPARATION TIME
10 minutes

COOKING TIME
10 minutes, plus 15 minutes heat-processing

STORAGE
up to 2 years

MAKES
2 x 500 ml (17 fl oz/2 cup) jars

500 g (1 lb 2 oz) long green chillies, washed
2 teaspoons black peppercorns
2 teaspoons coriander, fennel or cumin seeds
500 ml (17 fl oz/2 cups) white wine vinegar
110 g (3¾ oz/½ cup) caster (superfine) sugar
1 teaspoon salt

First sterilise your jars (see page 250) and allow to cool.

Pierce each chilli with a sharp knife, so the brine can get inside and pickle them. Place a teaspoon of peppercorns and seeds in the bottom of each sterilised jar, then pack in the chillies (see page 252 for more on packing techniques).

Make a brine by putting the vinegar, sugar, salt and 250 ml (9 fl oz/1 cup) water into a small non-reactive saucepan. Place over low heat, stirring to dissolve the sugar and salt. Once the sugar and salt have completely dissolved, let the brine simmer for a few minutes, then turn off the heat.

Pour the hot brine over the chillies, making sure they are completely submerged. Remove any air bubbles by gently tapping each jar on the work surface and sliding a butter knife or chopstick around the inside to release any hidden air pockets. You may need to add more chillies or brine after doing this (the liquid should reach about 1 cm/½ in from the top of the jar). Wipe the rims of the jars with paper towel and seal.

Heat-process (see page 255) for 15 minutes, then store in a cool, dark place.

PREPARATION TIME
20 minutes

STORAGE
up to 2 weeks

MAKES
about 750 ml
(26 fl oz/3 cups)

QUICK PICKLED RADISHES

The prettiest pickle we make, this one works better as a quick pickle that is kept in the fridge for a week, rather than being bottled and stored for months on end. The texture of pickled radishes deteriorates quite quickly – they go rubbery and lose their colour – but this method keeps them crunchy. These can be used in salads, eaten with bread and butter, on a ploughman's plate (see page 160) or in light, Asian-inspired dishes.

We like to keep the tails on our radishes. If your radishes are small, keep them whole; if they're larger, halve or quarter them.

400 g (14 oz) radishes, about 2 bunches, washed

QUICK-PICKLING BRINE
500 ml (17 fl oz/2 cups) white wine vinegar
2 tablespoons caster (superfine) sugar
pinch of salt
4 allspice berries
6 black peppercorns
2 bay leaves

For the quick-pickling brine, put the vinegar, sugar, salt and 250 ml (9 fl oz/ 1 cup) water into a small non-reactive saucepan. Place over low heat, stirring to dissolve the sugar and salt. Once the sugar and salt have completely dissolved, add the allspice, peppercorns and bay leaves and simmer the brine for a couple of minutes.

Put the radishes into a glass container with a lid. Pour over the hot brine, then leave to cool before storing in the fridge for a week or so. Although these pickled radishes can be eaten the next day, their flavour is better after a few days in the fridge.

HOT PINK TURNIPS

Jaimee is Cornersmith's resident fermenter (see page 256 for her tips and advice on the process). For this ferment, she was inspired by a classic Lebanese pickle. The hot pink colour comes from the beetroot – and the longer you leave the turnips to ferment, the more the colour will develop. Although there are no added spices, fermented turnips alone are surprisingly full of flavour. Feel free to tweak this to your own taste: you could add coriander seeds, fennel seeds, cleaned coriander (cilantro) roots, peppercorns (black or pink), or a whole peeled garlic clove. Serve with meats, falafel and all Middle Eastern dishes.

PREPARATION TIME
20 minutes, plus 4 days fermenting

COOKING TIME
20 minutes

STORAGE
up to 6 months

MAKES
2 x 500 ml (17 fl oz/2 cup) jars

1½ teaspoons salt
1 beetroot (beet), peeled and cut in half
500 g (1 lb 2 oz) turnips

To make a brine, put 500 ml (17 fl oz/2 cups) of water and the salt in a non-reactive saucepan. Bring to the boil, then add one half of the beetroot and simmer for 20 minutes. Set aside and leave the brine to cool to room temperature.

Meanwhile, sterilise your jars (see page 250).

Peel the turnips and cut into strips about 6 cm x 1 cm (2½ in x ½ in). Cut the other half of the beetroot into 1 cm (½ in) cubes.

When the brine and jars are both cool, pack the turnips into the jars, adding a few cubes of beetroot to each jar (see page 252 for more on packing techniques). Remove the beetroot half from the brine, then fill the jars with the brine, making sure the vegetables are completely covered. Wipe the rims of the jars and seal.

Let the jars sit at room temperature (but out of direct sunlight) for 2–4 days. During this time, the lids will start to pop up, which is a sign of the fermenting process (see pages 256–259 for more details). Transfer the jars to the fridge and leave for a week before opening, then use within 6 months.

PREPARATION TIME
20 minutes, plus at least 1 hour salting (or overnight) and 20 minutes bottling

COOKING TIME
1 hour, plus 10 minutes heat-processing

STORAGE
up to 12 months

MAKES
4 x 300 ml (10½ fl oz) jars

GREEN TOMATO RELISH

Red tomatoes aren't really at their best until summer is in full swing, so this is a great way to get your tomato relish fix in the springtime. We serve this in the cafe with poached eggs, or on ham sandwiches and wraps. It's also nice on toast – put a dollop on top of fresh ricotta and sprinkle with herbs.

1.5 kg (3 lb 5 oz) green tomatoes, cut into 1 cm (½ in) cubes
2 tablespoons salt
60 ml (2 fl oz/¼ cup) vegetable oil or olive oil
100 g (3½ oz) ginger, thinly sliced or finely grated
2 teaspoons brown mustard seeds
½ teaspoon freshly ground black pepper
1 teaspoon ground coriander
½ teaspoon ground turmeric
1 teaspoon ground fenugreek
1 kg (2 lb 4 oz) onions, thinly sliced
110 g (3¾ oz/½ cup) caster (superfine) sugar
500 ml (17 fl oz/2 cups) white wine vinegar

Put the green tomatoes into a bowl and sprinkle with the salt. Mix well and leave to sit for at least an hour – you can leave them to sit overnight if you have the time. This draws out excess moisture from the tomatoes.

Heat the vegetable oil in a large, heavy-based saucepan over medium heat. Add the ginger and spices and stir until fragrant. Add the onions and sauté for about 15 minutes or until they have collapsed – you want the onions to be very soft and sweet.

Drain off any excess liquid from the salted tomatoes, then add the tomatoes to the pan and stir to mix well. Lower the heat and cook until the tomatoes have softened, then add the sugar and vinegar, stirring to dissolve the sugar. Slowly bring to the boil and let the relish simmer, uncovered, for about 40 minutes, or until the desired consistency is reached: the relish should be glossy and thick, with no puddles of liquid on the surface.

Meanwhile, sterilise your jars (see page 250).

Taste the relish and add more salt, if needed, then set aside to cool for 10 minutes. Carefully ladle the hot relish into the hot jars. Wipe the rims of the jars with paper towel, then seal and heat-process (see page 255) for 10 minutes.

Leave to cool before storing in a cool, dark place for up to 12 months.

GREEN TOMATO HOT SAUCE

Our green tomato hot sauce is delicious, and makes a great alternative to Tabasco. We use it all the time when we've made something kid-friendly that needs a lift for the adults. You can also mix it through vinaigrettes for a salad dressing. It's best to make enough to last you for the whole year. Try making a red version with red tomatoes and red chillies later in the season.

750 g (1 lb 10 oz) green tomatoes, roughly chopped
juice and finely grated zest of 4 limes
125 g (4½ oz) green chillies, roughly chopped
125 g (4½ oz) onions, roughly chopped
2 large garlic cloves, roughly chopped
¾ teaspoon salt
125 ml (4 fl oz/½ cup) white wine vinegar

First sterilise your bottles (see page 250).

Put all the ingredients except the vinegar into a food processor and blend into a thin, smooth paste.

Pour the paste into a saucepan and add the vinegar. Bring to the boil and let it bubble for a few minutes, then carefully pour into the hot sterilised bottles. Seal and heat-process (see page 255) for 10 minutes.

Leave to cool before storing in a cool, dark place for up to 12 months.

PREPARATION TIME
20 minutes

COOKING TIME
5 minutes,
plus 10 minutes
heat-processing

STORAGE
up to 12 months

MAKES
5 x 250 ml
(9 fl oz/1 cup)
bottles

PREPARATION TIME
30 minutes

COOKING TIME
1½ hours

STORAGE
up to 12 months

MAKES
4 x 300 ml
(10½ fl oz) jars

CHILLI JAM

This is a sweet, spicy jam that makes a perfect replacement for sweet chilli sauce. Try it in marinades for sticky barbecued chicken wings or pork ribs, or with ricotta and salami in a sandwich. We use long red chillies and keep the seeds in, as they generally have plenty of heat without being too fiery, but this is also great with green chillies.

100 ml (3½ fl oz) vegetable oil
500 g (1 lb 2 oz) onions, thinly sliced
1 teaspoon ground coriander
1 teaspoon ground cumin
1 kg (2 lb 4 oz) long red chillies, thinly sliced
500 ml (17 fl oz/2 cups) white wine vinegar
750 g (1 lb 10 oz) caster (superfine) sugar

Pour the vegetable oil into a shallow, wide heavy-based pan over medium heat. Add the onions and sauté for about 15 minutes or until they are soft and sweet but not coloured. Stir in the coriander, cumin and chillies, reduce the heat to low and cook for another 15 minutes, stirring regularly to prevent the mixture sticking, or until the chillies are very soft. (The chillies and onions need to be very soft to prevent them from becoming candied once the sugar is added.)

Add the vinegar and 500 ml (17 fl oz/2 cups) water, stir well, then cook over medium heat for 10 minutes. Add the sugar, stirring to dissolve, then cook for 30–40 minutes or until setting point (see page 250) is reached, stirring occasionally to prevent sticking.

Meanwhile, sterilise your jars (see page 250).

When your chilli jam has reached setting point, turn off the heat and allow to cool slightly, then carefully fill the hot jars with the hot jam. Remove any air bubbles by gently tapping each jar on the work surface and sliding a butter knife or chopstick around the inside to release any hidden air pockets. Wipe the rims with a clean cloth and seal. Store in a cool, dark place for up to 12 months.

FRANCA'S CHEESECAKE

We seem to have lots of lovely German women working for us at Cornersmith. This recipe comes from Franca, and is a German version of a cheesecake, made with fresh cheese. We make it using Kristen's quark, which is a soft, white, un-aged cheese similar to cottage cheese, made without rennet. In Germany, quark is readily available, and here you may be able to get it at health food stores and delis, but if you can't find any, use ricotta instead.

PREPARATION TIME
30 minutes, plus at least 30 minutes resting

COOKING TIME
40 minutes, plus a few hours chilling

MAKES
1 x 24 cm (9½ in) cheesecake

500 g (1 lb 2 oz) quark or ricotta
finely grated zest of 1 lemon, plus a squeeze of juice, if you like
1 vanilla bean, split and seeds scraped
2 free-range eggs, separated
1 tablespoon cornflour (cornstarch)
60 g (2¼ oz) caster (superfine) sugar

SWEET PASTRY
125 g (4½ oz) unsalted butter, at room temperature
90 g (3¼ oz) caster (superfine) sugar
1 free-range egg
2 teaspoons vanilla essence or 1 vanilla bean, split and seeds scraped
250 g (9 oz/1⅔ cups) plain (all-purpose) flour
1 free-range egg yolk, mixed with 1 tablespoon water

For the sweet pastry, use an electric mixer to cream the butter and sugar until well combined, then beat in the egg and vanilla essence or seeds. Add the flour and a pinch of salt and mix until just combined – don't over-mix. Wrap the pastry in plastic wrap and chill in the fridge for at least 30 minutes.

Preheat the oven to 180°C (350°F/gas mark 4) and grease a 24 cm (9½ in) loose-based tart (flan) tin.

Roll out the pastry to a thickness of 3 mm (⅛ in) and use to line the tart tin, gently pressing it into the corners of the tin before trimming off the excess pastry. Use a fork to lightly prick the base, then line the pastry case with baking paper and baking beans (or raw rice or lentils). Blind-bake for 10 minutes, then remove the baking paper and beans. Brush the pastry with some of the egg yolk and water mixture just to lightly coat, then bake for another 7 minutes or until golden. Remove from the oven and leave to cool on a wire rack. Reduce the oven temperature to 170°C (325°F/gas mark 3).

Combine the cheese with the lemon zest and vanilla seeds. Whisk in the egg yolks, then sift in the cornflour and mix well. In another bowl, whisk the egg whites until soft peaks form, then gradually add the sugar and keep whisking until stiff and glossy. (For an extra lemony flavour, add a squeeze of lemon juice.) Gently fold the egg white mixture into the cheese mixture until just combined, then spoon into the pastry case, ensuring the top is smooth and even.

Bake the cheesecake for about 20 minutes or until risen and golden brown around the edges, but still a bit wobbly in the middle. Leave to cool completely, then chill in the fridge for a few hours before serving.

PREPARATION TIME
10 minutes, plus
30–60 minutes
steeping

COOKING TIME
15 minutes

SERVES 4

RHUBARB & HIBISCUS

This recipe makes delicious poached fruit and a versatile syrup at the same time. The combination of rhubarb and hibiscus tea creates such a startling red syrup that it almost looks artificial! Hibiscus tea is very high in vitamin C and adds a hint of acidity to the sweetness. You should be able to buy loose hibiscus tea at specialist tea shops and wholefood stores, but if you can only find it in bags, break them open and measure out 2 tablespoons of tea.

Choose a pan that will hold the rhubarb in a single layer, or it might overcook and lose its shape. If you don't have a pan wide enough, just poach the rhubarb in two or more batches. This recipe makes quite a lot of syrup to ensure there's enough to cover the rhubarb. Use the fruit over muesli or ice cream, and any left-over syrup is great in cocktails or as an alternative to the pomegranate syrup on page 142.

2 tablespoons hibiscus tea leaves
2 litres (70 fl oz/8 cups) boiling water
1 kg (2 lb 4 oz) caster (superfine) sugar
150 ml (5 fl oz) lemon juice – from about 2–3 lemons
500 g (1 lb 2 oz) trimmed rhubarb stalks,
    cut into 5–6 cm (2–2½ in) lengths

Choose a non-reactive saucepan that will hold the rhubarb in a single layer. Put the hibiscus tea in the pan and pour over the boiling water, then cover and leave to steep for 30–60 minutes.

Add the sugar and lemon juice to the pan and place over low heat. Slowly bring to a simmer, stirring every now and then to dissolve the sugar. Once the sugar has completely dissolved, let the syrup simmer and infuse for about 10 minutes.

Bring the syrup to a rapid boil and add the rhubarb, then reduce the heat to medium and let it simmer for 2–3 minutes or until the rhubarb is almost soft. Turn off the heat and let the rhubarb sit in the pan – the residual heat will soften the rhubarb while keeping its shape.

If you're not serving this straightaway, you can let the rhubarb cool down in the syrup, then refrigerate it, covered with syrup, for up to 5 days.

If you want to preserve the left-over syrup, bring it to the boil in a non-reactive saucepan and simmer for about 15 minutes or until thickened. Carefully pour the hot syrup into hot sterilised bottles or jars (see page 250) and seal immediately. Store in a cool, dark place for up to 2 years.

MULBERRY COMPOTE

PREPARATION TIME
15 minutes,
plus 1–12 hours macerating

COOKING TIME
30 minutes

MAKES
about 500 ml
(17 fl oz/2 cups)

It was mulberry season when we first opened Cornersmith, and there are mulberry trees everywhere in Marrickville. They hang over fences and stain the footpaths purple. For a while there we'd pull over every time we saw a fruit-filled tree and make the kids stand on the roof of the car to fill up buckets. Eventually we took to keeping a ladder and buckets in the back of our van for the duration of the mulberry season!

We make mulberry compote for our milkshakes (see page 118) and serve it on top of muesli at the cafe. You can also spoon this over ice cream or use it as a sweet braise for pork or gamey meats. It will keep for up to a week in the fridge.

750 g (1 lb 10 oz) mulberries, stems removed
75 g (2½ oz/⅓ cup) caster (superfine) or raw sugar
juice and finely grated zest of 1 orange
2 tablespoons honey

Put the mulberries into a non-reactive saucepan, lightly crushing them with your hands as you go. Sprinkle over the sugar and mix well, then leave to sit for at least 1 hour or up to 12 hours.

Add the orange juice and zest to the pan, along with the honey, then place over low heat. Stir until the honey and sugar have completely dissolved, then simmer for 20 minutes or until the berries have really broken down. Taste for sweetness, adding more sugar if necessary.

At this stage you can leave the compote as is or purée it with a stick blender for a smoother texture. We tend to blitz this one, as mulberry seeds can often be quite tough and they don't break down during the cooking process.

MULBERRY YOGHURT ICE BLOCKS

PREPARATION TIME
10 minutes, plus overnight freezing

MAKES
12 ice blocks

This is an easy recipe for the warmer months. We made these a lot for our kids when they were little, and now they make them on their own. You can do this with any kind of fruit compote, such as apricot and cardamom on page 118.

500 ml (17 fl oz/2 cups) mulberry compote (see above)
520 g (1 lb 2½ oz/2 cups) natural yoghurt
honey, to taste – optional

Stir the mulberry compote into the yoghurt. Taste and add honey if you think it needs it – the mulberry compote already has honey in it, remember.

Pour into ice-block moulds, then add paddle-pop sticks and freeze overnight.

THE LEMONADE STALL

Every year, Cornersmith teams up with our kids' school, Dulwich Hill Primary, to raise funds for their edible garden and the students who plant and tend it, aka the Dully Green Thumbs. Over a weekend, we hold a 'poached egg roll drive'. The rolls come with Dully Green Thumbs greens, so the kids get to see the fruits of their hard work eaten and enjoyed by the community. All profits go towards funding a specially trained teacher and garden supplies, and hopefully towards inspiring many more Dully Green Thumbs.

For the past couple of years, our kids and their school friends have also run a lemonade stand outside the cafe. It goes something like this: Alex spends a hilarious day at the school, teaching a hundred Year One students how to make lemon cordial from their backyard lemons, supplemented with whatever we have left at the picklery from our trading (see page 194). Then, at the stall, the kids add fizzy water to turn the cordial into lemonade.

We do this on the same weekend as Marrickville Festival, so it's a very busy and rewarding time for the community. It's great to see so many connections being made – between the kids, the school and local people and businesses. There's nothing like seeing the Marrickville spirit in action!

CORNERSMITH POACHED EGG ROLL

PREPARATION TIME
10 minutes

COOKING TIME
5 minutes

SERVES 4

The Cornersmith poached egg roll has been a staple on our menu since we first opened. It's our take on the classic cafe bacon and egg roll. The roll changes with every seasonal menu, depending on the slaw we have on, the chutney or pickle we're using and the cured meat Feather and Bone, our meat suppliers, have provided us.

This is more of a suggestion than a recipe. Any of the slaws in the book (see pages 42, 82 and 203) would work well, as would the chutneys and sliced pickles. Or just use what you have in the fridge.

- 2–3 handfuls leafy greens plus the juice of ½ lemon and 2 tablespoons olive oil or 2–3 large spoonfuls slaw
- 4 sourdough or ciabatta-style rolls, cut in half
- 4 teaspoons aioli (see page 97) or butter
- 4–8 slices of ham, salami or cheese
- 4 poached free-range eggs (see page 261) or soft-boiled eggs
- 4 tablespoons relish, chutney or pickles

If you're using leafy greens instead of slaw, put them in a bowl, season with salt and pepper and dress with the lemon juice and olive oil.

Lightly toast the rolls, then spread 1 teaspoon of aioli over the bottom half of each roll, place the meat or cheese on top and cover with the dressed leafy greens or slaw.

Sit the egg on the salad, followed by the relish, chutney or pickles. Top with the other half of the roll and eat straightaway.

PREPARATION TIME
40 minutes, plus cooling time

COOKING TIME
10 minutes

MAKES
2 litres (70 fl oz/ 8 cups)

LEMON CORDIAL

Here's the tried-and-tested recipe from our kids' lemonade stall.

880 g (1 lb 15 oz/4 cups) caster (superfine) sugar
about 2 kg (4 lb 8 oz) lemons

Give your bottles a good soapy wash and a rinse.

Tip the sugar into a saucepan and pour in 1 litre (35 fl oz/4 cups) of water. Put the pan on the stove over low heat (get a grown-up to help!) and stir until all the sugar has dissolved. Bring to the boil and cook for 3 minutes, then turn off the heat and let the sugar syrup cool down.

Cut your lemons in half and squeeze the juice into a jug – you will need 1 litre (35 fl oz/4 cups) of lemon juice.

Once the syrup is cool, add the lemon juice and mix. Pour the lemon cordial into the bottles using a funnel. Put the lids on and keep in the fridge – the cordial will last for up to a week.

Once your cordial is made, it's really easy to make a yummy lemonade drink. Fill a glass with ice, pour over 60 ml (2 fl oz/¼ cup) of cordial, then top up with plain or sparkling water. If you like, you can also add a slice of lemon, some mint or any herbs from your garden.

Invite your friends over to run a lemonade stall!

SUMMER

PEACH & LIME JAM

A fresh, light and tangy jam that we teach in our jam-making workshops. The peaches can easily be substituted with other stone fruit, such as nectarines or apricots, and the limes with lemons. More lime (or lemon) zest can be added too, according to your taste. Make enough to last you through the year – it's great popping open a jar of this on a wintry morning.

PREPARATION TIME
15 minutes

COOKING TIME
50 minutes

STORAGE
2 years

MAKES
4–5 x 300 ml (10½ fl oz) jars

2 kg (4 lb 8 oz) peaches
1 kg (2 lb 4 oz) caster (superfine) sugar
juice and finely grated zest of 4 limes

Halve the peaches (or your choice of fruit), remove the stones, then chop into 2 cm (¾ in) chunks.

Put the peaches and 1 litre (35 fl oz/4 cups) of water into a large saucepan over low heat and simmer slowly until the peaches are soft and falling apart, about 30 minutes.

Meanwhile, sterilise your jars (see page 250).

Add the sugar to the peaches and stir until completely dissolved, then stir in the lime juice and half of the zest. Turn up the heat and boil rapidly for about 15 minutes or until setting point is reached (see page 250). Keep an eye on the jam while it's cooking, and stir occasionally to prevent it burning. Remove from the heat, stir in the remaining lime zest and let the jam sit for a few minutes.

Carefully pour the hot jam into the hot jars. Wipe the rims with a clean damp cloth or paper towel, then put the lids on.

Store in a cool, dark place for up to 2 years. Once opened, refrigerate and use within 6–8 weeks.

PREPARATION TIME
15 minutes

COOKING TIME
10 minutes

SERVES 4

ZUCCHINI & FARRO SALAD WITH TOASTED HAZELNUTS

Farro is a spelt-like grain with a nutty flavour and chewy texture. Using it in a salad like this one makes for a great vegetarian summertime meal. Make sure you get the pearled sort: this has been de-hulled and undergone a process that makes it easier to cook and digest – it doesn't need soaking, you just boil it for 8–10 minutes. We like to cook grains al dente, so they retain their shape and nutrients. If you can't find farro, pearled barley is a good substitute.

While we love this as a main, it is also a great accompaniment to meats and fish. If you don't have hazelnuts on hand, almonds or toasted seeds will work just as well.

200 g (7 oz/1 cup) farro (pearled spelt), rinsed and drained
2 zucchini (courgettes), thinly sliced lengthways using a mandoline or very sharp knife
½ red onion, thinly sliced
6 prunes, pitted and finely chopped
50 ml (1¾ fl oz) apple balsamic vinegar, regular balsamic vinegar or sherry vinegar
½ teaspoon dijon mustard
60 ml (2 fl oz/¼ cup) vegetable oil
60 ml (2 fl oz/¼ cup) olive oil
large handful (¾ cup) mixed herb sprigs, such as mint, parsley and dill
50 g (1¾ oz/⅓ cup) toasted hazelnuts, roughly chopped

Put the farro into a large saucepan of salted boiling water. When the water comes back to the boil, reduce the heat and let it simmer for 8–10 minutes, or until the farro is cooked but still has a bite to it. Drain.

Meanwhile, combine the zucchini, onion and prunes in a bowl and add a pinch of salt to soften the raw zucchini.

To make a dressing for the salad, combine the vinegar, mustard and both the oils in a screw-top jar and season with salt and pepper. Put the lid on and shake well to emulsify.

Add the cooked farro to the zucchini, onion and prunes. Tear the herbs into smaller pieces, then add them to the salad along with the dressing, and toss gently to combine.

Place the salad in a serving bowl or on plates and scatter over the hazelnuts.

TOMATO & FIG SALAD

PREPARATION TIME
10 minutes

SERVES 4

Here is Sabine's famous, quintessential summer salad that we serve on our annual Tomato Day (see page 98), during our summer workshops, and in the cafe. By the end of summer, both tomatoes and figs are at their peak: ripe, tasty and abundant. We eat as much as we can, then miss them for the rest of the year.

50 ml (1¾ fl oz) sherry vinegar
finely grated zest of ½ lemon
1 teaspoon sumac
125 ml (4 fl oz/½ cup) olive oil
8–10 small or 5 large ripe tomatoes, such as ox-heart, cut into quarters or chunky pieces
4–6 figs, depending on size, cut into quarters
2 tablespoons tarragon leaves, small ones left whole, larger ones chopped
120 g (4¾ oz) labneh (see page 37)

To make a dressing for the salad, combine the sherry vinegar, lemon zest, sumac and olive oil in a screw-top jar. Season with salt and pepper, then put on the lid and shake well to mix.

Arrange the tomatoes and figs on a serving plate, seasoning them lightly with salt and pepper. Scatter over the tarragon and place dollops of labneh around the plate. Finish the salad by drizzling the dressing evenly over the tomatoes, figs and labneh.

PREPARATION TIME
10 minutes

COOKING TIME
2 minutes

SERVES 4

RICOTTA & FIGS ON TOAST WITH HONEY & FENNEL FLOWERS

The perfect weekend breakfast, and a staple dish at the cafe. We vary the soft cheese (labneh, quark, goat's cheese, ricotta), depending on what Kristen is making; and the fruit depending on what our fruit-and-veg supplier Shane thinks looks good at the market, what's been dropped off for trading, or what's at the height of its season, so it's ripe and full of flavour.

As fennel flowers grow wild along the Cooks River and the railway lines in Marrickville, Shane refuses to let us buy them and instructs us where to forage. We preserve the flowers and stems in honey to make them last longer and to give the honey a subtle aniseed flavour. You might be able to find some near your home as well; other edible flowers will also look as pretty on the plate – just make sure their flavour isn't too intense or bitter. If you can't find any edible flowers, use toasted nuts and seeds, or a warm spice like cinnamon or nutmeg instead.

8 slices good-quality sourdough bread
300 g (10½ oz) ricotta
8–10 figs, halved or quartered, depending on size
4 tablespoons honey
2 fennel flowers or other edible flowers, picked
   (or a pinch of ground nutmeg or cinnamon)

Toast the slices of bread, then spread generously with the ricotta.

Arrange the cut figs over the bread, drizzle with honey and sprinkle with the flowers.

PREPARATION TIME
20 minutes, plus at least 20 minutes (or overnight) pickling

SERVES
4 as a side salad, or 2–3 as a light meal

RED CABBAGE, PICKLED CORN, CHILLI & CORIANDER SLAW

We always have some sort of slaw on the menu. Sabine loves coming up with interesting combinations of seasonal vegetables and herbs. So many vegetables are delicious used in salads – zucchini (courgettes), brussels sprouts, fennel, beetroot (beets) – but people don't often think to shred them and eat them raw. A mandoline will give you lovely fine ribbons, but if you don't have one just use a sharp knife and slice as thinly as you can. Looking for alternatives to green leaves for the cafe menu, we started exploring raw vegetable slaws, and it turned into a real adventure. There are so many variations you can try, and the textures and colours have become an important part of the aesthetic of our food.

The red cabbage in this dish gives it a beautiful colour in the bowl. We use this in a wrap (see page 89), but it's also great as a side for eggs or fish, or to take along to a barbecue.

- 1 corn cob, kernels cut off the cob
- 2 teaspoons sea salt
- 75 g (2½ oz/⅓ cup) caster (superfine) sugar
- 125 ml (4 fl oz/½ cup) white wine vinegar or apple cider vinegar
- 250 ml (9 fl oz/1 cup) boiling water, cooled down for 5 minutes
- ¼ red cabbage (around 400 g/14 oz), tough outer leaves and core removed, thinly sliced using a mandoline or very sharp knife
- 1 Lebanese (short) cucumber, sliced into ribbons or any other shape you like
- ½ red chilli, seeds removed, finely chopped
- ½ small red onion, thinly sliced
- juice and finely grated zest of 1 lime
- 80 ml (2½ fl oz/⅓ cup) olive oil
- 2 teaspoons green tomato hot sauce (see page 51) or other hot sauce, such as Tabasco
- handful (½ cup, firmly packed) coriander (cilantro) leaves
- small handful (¼ cup) basil leaves

To pickle the corn, place the corn kernels in a heatproof bowl. In another bowl, stir the salt and sugar into the vinegar until dissolved. Add the cooled boiled water, then pour this liquid over the corn kernels. Leave to pickle for at least 20 minutes, or as long as overnight. Before use, drain the corn kernels, keeping the pickling liquid aside.

Combine the cabbage, cucumber, chilli, onion and drained corn in a large bowl.

To make a dressing, put the lime juice and zest, olive oil and hot chilli sauce in a screw-top jar and add 2 teaspoons of the pickling liquid. Season with salt and pepper, then put the lid on the jar and shake well to mix.

Add enough dressing to the vegetables to coat them evenly. (Any left-over dressing will keep in the jar in the fridge for up to a week.) Add the herbs, toss gently and serve the slaw in a bowl or on a platter.

GREEN BEAN, BABY COS & NASHI PEAR SALAD WITH MISO DRESSING

PREPARATION TIME
15 minutes

COOKING TIME
5 minutes

SERVES 2–4

The miso dressing really makes this salad. Sabine teaches salad-making workshops at the picklery, focusing on seasonal choices and interesting combinations of vegetables, grains and flavours. She also makes delicious and unexpected dressings (see page 260), and any good salad-maker knows how important it is to have an array of dressings under your belt.

During bean season, you can try this recipe with all different types of beans. Nashi pears are in season during late summer here, but if you can't get hold of them, use any variety of pears. We use baby cos lettuce because it is crunchier than its big brother, but normal-sized cos would also work, of course.

300 g (10½ oz) green beans
1 baby cos (romaine) lettuce
2 tablespoons white miso paste
1 teaspoon grated ginger
1 teaspoon honey
1 teaspoon dijon mustard
2 tablespoons lime juice
60 ml (2 fl oz/¼ cup) grapeseed or other vegetable oil
large handful (¾ cup) mint leaves
1 nashi pear, core removed, thinly sliced
2 teaspoons toasted sesame seeds (see page 261)

Blanch the green beans in a large saucepan of boiling salted water for 5 minutes or until the beans are tender but still have a bite to them. Refresh under cold running water and drain. If the beans are very long, cut them in half.

Separate the lettuce leaves, then wash and dry them well, ideally using a salad spinner. Tear into bite-sized pieces.

To make the dressing, mix the miso, ginger, honey, mustard, lime juice and 2 tablespoons of water with a whisk until smooth. Slowly whisk in the oil until combined.

Tear the mint leaves into smaller pieces. In a large bowl, combine the green beans, lettuce leaves, pear and half of the mint. Add just enough dressing to coat the salad.

Place the salad in a serving bowl, then garnish with the rest of the mint and the toasted sesame seeds. Drizzle with a little more dressing and serve.

PREPARATION TIME
15 minutes

COOKING TIME
25 minutes

SERVES
3–4, depending
how it's served

SPICED PORK & VEAL WITH POMEGRANATE SYRUP

This is our version of Lebanese minced or ground meat. It's quite a peppery dish, but the heat is well balanced by the sweetness of pomegranate. If you've made a batch of the rhubarb on page 58, you can use the left-over syrup in place of the pomegranate syrup.

We use this spicy meat in a lunch wrap (see page 89), but it's also delicious mixed with torn herbs and sprinkled on white bean mash (see page 223) or served on top of a salad.

1 teaspoon black peppercorns
1 teaspoon allspice berries
½ teaspoon native pepperberries – optional
2 tablespoons vegetable oil
½ red onion, finely chopped
1 garlic clove, finely chopped
250 g (9 oz) minced (ground) pasture-raised pork
250 g (9 oz) minced (ground) pasture-raised veal
3 tablespoons pomegranate syrup (see page 142) or pomegranate molasses

To make the spice mix, use a spice grinder or pestle and mortar to grind the peppercorns, allspice and native pepperberries, if using, to a fine powder.

Heat 1 tablespoon of the vegetable oil in a frying pan over medium heat. Add the onion, garlic and a pinch of salt and cook for about 5 minutes or until they soften. Add 1 teaspoon of the spice mix and continue cooking until the spices are fragrant. Transfer the onion mixture to a plate, then rinse and dry the pan.

Put the pan back on the stove and turn the heat up to high. Add 2 teaspoons of the oil and half of both meats. Season with salt and add half of the remaining spice mix. Don't move the meat until it really starts to colour, then stir and cook for another 1–2 minutes. Remove the meat, rinse out the pan and repeat with the remaining oil, meats and spice mix.

When the second batch of meat is done, return the cooked onion mixture and the rest of the cooked meat to the pan. Add the pomegranate syrup and cook until the meat is cooked through and the syrup has almost evaporated, about 3–5 minutes.

NAAN BREAD WITH RED CABBAGE SLAW, SPICED PORK & VEAL & GREEN TOMATO RELISH

PREPARATION TIME
5–10 minutes

SERVES 4

We always have a wrap or flatbread on the menu at Cornersmith as a lighter alternative to a sandwich, and we generally keep ours vegetarian, with the meat as an optional extra. If you're making this for a lunch party, you can just put all the elements in bowls and let everyone assemble their own.

4 naan breads or similar flatbreads
½ quantity preserved lemon aioli (see page 97)
½ quantity red cabbage slaw (see page 82)
½ quantity spiced pork and veal (see page 86)
4 tablespoons green tomato relish (see page 50)

Briefly warm the naan breads in a sandwich press or a preheated 150°C (300°F/gas mark 2) oven.

Spread 1 teaspoon of aioli evenly over each bread, then top with slaw. Spoon some freshly cooked spiced pork and veal over the slaw and finish with a tablespoon of relish.

TOMATO & CHERRY GAZPACHO

PREPARATION TIME
20 minutes, plus at least 2 hours chilling

SERVES
4 as a small starter or 10–12 in little shot glasses at a drinks party

This cold soup is a union of two summer fruits, and the colour blows you away. Just make sure you use the best-quality olive oil, the tastiest tomatoes and the reddest cherries.

500 g (1 lb 2 oz) ripe tomatoes, roughly chopped
200 g (7 oz) cherries, stones removed
80 ml (2½ fl oz/⅓ cup) olive oil, plus extra to serve
1–2 tablespoons apple balsamic vinegar or regular balsamic vinegar
1 tablespoon chervil or basil leaves

Put the tomatoes and cherries in a food processor or blender, then blend to a soupy texture. With the motor running, add the olive oil in a slow and steady stream. Keep blending until the soup is smooth and emulsified, then season with salt and pepper and add the vinegar to taste.

Pass the soup through a sieve into a jug or bowl, then chill in the fridge for at least 2 hours or as long as overnight.

Give the soup a good whisk before serving. Pour into cold bowls or glasses and drizzle a little olive oil on top, then garnish with chervil or torn basil leaves.

BARBECUED FISH WITH GRILLED CAPSICUM, HERB SALAD & PRESERVED LEMON AIOLI

PREPARATION TIME
20 minutes

COOKING TIME
20 minutes

SERVES 4

We always use sustainable fish like Spanish mackerel or large whiting for this. It makes a great outdoors meal, as everything can be cooked on the barbecue.

- 4 x 250–300 g (9–10½ oz) mackerel or whiting, cleaned and gutted
- 1–1½ teaspoons fennel, orange and chilli salt (see page 33)
- 8 thyme sprigs
- 4 garlic cloves, 2 sliced very thinly and 2 left whole
- 125 ml (4 fl oz/½ cup) olive oil
- 2 medium or 3 small red capsicums (peppers), seeds and membrane removed, cut into wide strips
- 1½ tablespoons apple balsamic vinegar or regular balsamic vinegar
- 2 large handfuls soft herb leaves, such as chervil, parsley and basil
- 1 tablespoon toasted almonds (see page 261), roughly chopped
- 1 lemon – optional
- 2–3 tablespoons preserved lemon aioli (see page 97)

Preheat the barbecue to medium. Wash the fish under cold running water, then thoroughly pat dry, both inside and out. Season the bellies (insides) of the fish with some of the fennel, orange and chilli salt, then stuff with the thyme sprigs and sliced garlic. Close the belly of each fish with a toothpick to keep the flavourings inside, then drizzle both sides with olive oil and set aside.

Put the whole garlic cloves and a large pinch of salt in a mortar and grind to a paste with the pestle. Stir through 1½ tablespoons of olive oil, then brush all over the capsicum strips. Grill on the barbecue for 3–4 minutes on each side or until soft and slightly charred. Transfer to a bowl and set aside.

Turn the barbecue up to high. Season the outside of the fish with some more of the fennel, orange and chilli salt, and place on the grill. After 4–5 minutes, lower the heat to medium and try to loosen the fish from the grill: it should be easy to lift them up; if not, they need a bit longer.

Carefully turn the fish and cook for 2–3 minutes on the other side, until the fish is cooked – the flesh should give when you press it lightly. Transfer the fish to a plate and set aside to rest for 2–3 minutes.

Meanwhile, sprinkle the vinegar and about 2 tablespoons of the olive oil over the grilled capsicum. Add the herbs and almonds and season with some salt and pepper, if needed, then mix everything together very gently.

Serve the fish on plates (with a squeeze of lemon juice, if you like), with the capsicum and herb salad and preserved lemon aioli on the side.

PRESERVED LEMON AIOLI

PREPARATION TIME
10 minutes

MAKES
about 250 ml
(9 fl oz/1 cup)

Every time Alex teaches a preserving class, she gets asked what to do with preserved lemons, and this is one of the many things we've tried. Sabine makes amazing flavoured aiolis: quince, smoked potato, corn. In this one, the saltiness and freshness of the preserved lemons lightens and lifts the aioli, giving it a summery crispness. An easy sauce to make, this is delicious with fish and seafood.

2 free-range egg yolks
1½ teaspoons white wine vinegar
½ teaspoon dijon mustard
½ garlic clove, finely chopped
¼ preserved lemon (see page 214), rind only, finely chopped
250 ml (9 fl oz/1 cup) vegetable oil

Put the egg yolks, vinegar, mustard, garlic and preserved lemon in a food processor or blender and season with salt (go easy on the salt, as the preserved lemon will be very salty).

Start the machine and add the vegetable oil in a thin, steady stream – do this really slowly, or the aioli may split. Blend until the mixture is thick and creamy, then check the seasoning.

Use immediately or store in the fridge for up to 5 days.

TOMATO DAY

Tomato Day is a time for family and friends to get together and make enough preserved tomato goods to last until the next season. A long-standing tradition in Italian communities across Australia, its popularity is spreading, and so we started running Tomato Day workshops at the picklery.

Tomatoes only taste good in season, and as a result many of us rely heavily on tinned tomatoes. Unfortunately, though, Australian tinned varieties can taste metallic and contain unnecessary additives; imported ones travel many food miles, and buying them does nothing to support local farmers.

Cornersmith's annual Tomato Day had humble beginnings. Jaimee and Alex bought 100 kg (about 220 lb) of tomatoes from the markets and spent a very long day in a tiny Pyrmont apartment with four small, restless children. On that first Tomato Day, they made enough bottled tomatoes to last two families until the following summer. Jaimee filled her linen press with bottles and kept her sheets and towels in buckets on the floor!

The following year we upgraded the venue to the cafe, after hours, where six picklers made short work of our haul of tomatoes. The only problem was the mismatch between the enormous 44-gallon drum we were using for our heat-processing and the tiny outdoor gas burner that was all we had to heat it. We sat there until 3 am waiting for the water to boil.

In its third year, Tomato Day was held at the picklery, and it was a great success! We had plenty of hands on deck: Sabine, Jaimee, Maddy, Franca, Jeannie and her son, Shane (our veggie guy) and his family, our kids and us. Everyone got their hands red! This time we divided our spoils into bottled tomatoes, some passata and a batch of ketchup. The adults cried chopping onions, while the kids sat on the front step picking basil leaves and eating ice cream. Later on, they really got into crushing the tomatoes by hand. And at the end of the day, we all sat down to a tomato feast. Sabine made us fresh fettuccine with passata, and a tomato and fig salad (see page 77) topped with Kristen's labneh (see page 37). We were definitely ready for a drink, but we'd preserved enough tomatoes for spaghetti, baked beans and bloody marys to keep us going through the winter. We're already looking forward to next year ...

BOTTLED TOMATOES

This is how you preserve tomatoes when you don't want to have to rely on tinned ones. It's a sustainable and economical alternative – and once you taste them, you won't want to go back. Make enough to tide you over until next summer. We'd suggest buying about 20 kg (44 lb) of tomatoes and making a day of it. Or, if you're game and have some helping hands, double that amount.

PREPARATION TIME
a few hours, depending how many hands you have on deck – set aside a day

COOKING TIME
about 30 minutes, plus 40 minutes heat-processing

STORAGE
up to 12 months

MAKES
8–10 x 500 ml (17 fl oz/2 cup) jars

5 kg (11 lb 4 oz) tomatoes
ice – optional
160–200 ml (5¼–7 fl oz) lemon juice – about 6–7 lemons
about 175 g (6 oz) salt

Bring a large saucepan of water to the boil.

Using a small knife, score a cross in the base of each tomato, then cut out the core at the top without removing too much of the flesh. Fill a large bowl with cold water and ice, if you have it.

Once the water is boiling, put a kilo or so of tomatoes at a time into the boiling water. Leave for 1 minute, then remove with a slotted spoon and plunge into the icy water. Once cool, transfer to another bowl, then repeat with the rest of the tomatoes. Remove the skins from the tomatoes – they should slip off easily.

Sterilise your jars (see page 250). Leave them to cool completely, then put 1 tablespoon of lemon juice and 3 teaspoons of salt into each jar.

For whole bottled tomatoes, pack the jars full of tomatoes (see page 252 for packing techniques), then add enough cold water to reach 1 cm (½ in) from the top of the jar. Remove any air bubbles by gently tapping each jar on the work surface and sliding a butter knife or chopstick around the inside to release any hidden air pockets. You may need to add more water or tomatoes after doing this. Wipe the rims of the jars with a clean cloth or paper towel and seal. Heat-process (see page 255) for 40 minutes, then store in a cool, dark place for up to 12 months. Once opened, refrigerate and use within 3 days.

For crushed bottled tomatoes, chop your tomatoes into quarters, then place in a bowl and crush with a spoon or mallet. Once all the tomatoes are crushed, carefully spoon into the jars. Remove any air bubbles by gently tapping each jar on the work surface and sliding a butter knife or chopstick around the inside to release any hidden air pockets. You may need to add more crushed tomatoes after doing this (the liquid should reach about 1 cm/½ in from the top of the jar). Wipe the rims of the jars with a clean cloth or paper towel and seal. Heat-process (see page 255) for 40 minutes, then store in a cool, dark place for up to 12 months. Once opened, refrigerate and use within 3 days.

PREPARATION TIME
40 minutes, plus
30 minutes cooling

COOKING TIME
1¼ hours, plus
40 minutes
heat-processing

STORAGE
up to 12 months

MAKES
5 x 500 ml
(17 fl oz/2 cup) jars

TOMATO PASSATA

This is a great thing to make with your family and friends, and is well worth the effort. The best time to do it is at the end of summer, when there is a glut of cheap and tasty tomatoes. This recipe was inspired by our hero Pam ('Pam the Jam') Corbin, who teaches preserving at Hugh Fearnley-Whittingstall's River Cottage in Dorset (and to whom Alex owes all her marmalade-making skills!). Pam suggests roasting the ingredients to intensify the flavour of the passata. If you want this for more general usage, just leave out the basil. Quadruple this recipe and make winter meals a breeze.

5 kg (11 lb 4 oz) ripe red tomatoes, cut in half
500 g (1 lb 2 oz) brown onions, cut into chunks
1 bulb unbleached garlic, separated into cloves
125 ml (4 fl oz/½ cup) olive oil
1 tablespoon salt
1 teaspoon freshly ground black pepper
1 bunch basil, leaves picked and roughly torn

Preheat the oven to 180°C (350°F/gas mark 4). Spread out the tomatoes on two baking trays, then scatter over the onions. Peel the garlic cloves and smash with a pestle or the back of a wooden spoon, then scatter them over the tomatoes. Drizzle about 60 ml (2 fl oz/¼ cup) of the olive oil over each tray and sprinkle with the salt and pepper, then mix everything with a spoon or your hands. Roast for 1 hour, then leave to cool for half an hour.

Add the basil to the cooled roast tomato mixture, then pass through a mouli, passata machine or nylon sieve. Run the waste (seeds and skins) through the mouli a few times to extract as much juice and flavour as you can. Pour the passata into a non-reactive stockpot or large saucepan, place over medium heat and bring to the boil, then let it bubble for 5 minutes.

Meanwhile, sterilise your jars (see page 250).

When the jars are cool enough to handle, pour the hot passata into the hot jars. Remove any air bubbles by gently tapping each jar on the work surface and sliding a butter knife or chopstick around the inside to release any hidden air pockets. Wipe the rims of the jars with a clean cloth or paper towel and seal. Heat-process (see page 255) for 40 minutes, then store in a cool, dark place for up to 12 months. Once opened, refrigerate and use within 3 days.

PATRICE'S TOMATO KETCHUP

When Patrice joined the Cornersmith family, he gave us this recipe for tomato ketchup, and it immediately replaced the more time-consuming one we'd been using before. This ketchup is easy for the kids to help make, as well as being sweet and salty enough for them to never go back to the store-bought version. Add cayenne pepper, chilli or smoky paprika to spice things up.

PREPARATION TIME
40 minutes

COOKING TIME
3 hours, plus 10 minutes heat-processing

STORAGE
up to 2 years

MAKES
6 x 250 ml (9 fl oz) bottles

60 ml (2 fl oz/¼ cup) vegetable oil
3 large onions, roughly chopped
2.8 kg (6 lb 4 oz) tomatoes, roughly chopped
2 large granny smith apples, peeled and cubed
1 litre (35 fl oz/4 cups) white wine vinegar
80 g (2¾ oz/¼ cup) salt
1½ tablespoons ground cloves
1½ tablespoons ground ginger
1½ tablespoons ground coriander
280 g (10 oz/1¼ cups, firmly packed) brown sugar

Heat the vegetable oil in a large non-reactive saucepan over medium heat and sauté the onions for about 5 minutes until they soften.

Add all the remaining ingredients except the sugar, then reduce the heat to low and simmer for 2 hours, stirring occasionally. Add the sugar and simmer for another 30 minutes.

Remove from the heat and blitz with a stick blender. (If you want a very smooth consistency, pass the ketchup through a sieve, pressing down to extract as much liquid – and flavour – as possible.)

Place the pan of ketchup back on the stovetop over low heat, cover with a lid and simmer for 30 minutes.

Meanwhile, sterilise your bottles (see page 250). When the bottles are cool enough to handle, pour the hot ketchup into the hot bottles and seal immediately. Heat-process (see page 255) for 10 minutes, then store in a cool, dark place for up to 2 years. Once opened, refrigerate and use within 3 months.

PREPARATION TIME
30 minutes, plus at least 1 hour salting

COOKING TIME
2¾ hours, plus 10 minutes heat-processing

STORAGE
up to 12 months

MAKES
8 x 300 ml (10½ fl oz) jars

TOMATO & EGGPLANT CHUTNEY

This chutney really highlights the season. Both eggplants and tomatoes are plentiful and very cheap in the middle of summer, so make the most of them!

Because this recipe is low in vinegar, it's important to heat-process the chutney to extend its shelf life.

- 2 kg (4 lb 8 oz) tomatoes
- 2 tablespoons salt
- 2 kg (4 lb 8 oz) eggplants (aubergines)
- 250 ml (9 fl oz/1 cup) olive oil
- 3 tablespoons coriander seeds
- 2 tablespoons fenugreek seeds
- 2 tablespoons cumin seeds
- 1 tablespoon freshly ground black pepper
- 1 teaspoon cayenne pepper
- 1 teaspoon chilli flakes – optional
- 1 kg (2 lb 4 oz) brown onions, thinly sliced
- 220 g (7¾ oz/1 cup) caster (superfine) sugar
- 500 ml (17 fl oz/2 cups) red wine vinegar

Cut the tomatoes into 2 cm (¾ in) cubes and put them into a large colander set over a bowl. Sprinkle 1 tablespoon of the salt over the tomatoes and mix through, then leave to sit for at least 1 hour.

Meanwhile, preheat the oven to 220°C (425°F/gas mark 7) and line a roasting tin with baking paper. Prick the eggplants with a fork or skewer and rub with olive oil. Place in the tin and roast for 45 minutes or until the eggplants are soft and wrinkled. When the roasted eggplants are cool enough to handle, cut into 4 cm (1½ in) chunks and set aside.

Use a spice grinder or pestle and mortar to grind the coriander, fenugreek and cumin seeds to a fine powder, then stir the pepper, cayenne and chilli flakes into the spice mixture. Pour the remaining olive oil into a large saucepan over medium heat, then add the spice mixture and sauté until fragrant. Add the onions and sauté gently until they have completely softened; do not let them brown.

Pour away any liquid that has seeped from the eggplants, then add the tomatoes and eggplants to the pan. Stir well to make sure nothing is sticking, then turn down the heat and simmer for about 15 minutes to soften the tomatoes and eggplants slightly. Add the sugar and vinegar and stir until the sugar has completely dissolved. Cook over low–medium heat, uncovered, for 1½ hours or until a chutney consistency is reached (see page 256).

When the chutney is close to being ready, sterilise your jars (see page 250).

Take the chutney off the heat and let it sit for a few minutes, then fill the hot jars with the hot chutney. Remove any air bubbles by gently tapping each jar on the work surface and sliding a butter knife or chopstick around the inside to release any hidden air pockets. Wipe the rims of the jars with a clean cloth or paper towel and seal. Heat-process (see page 255) for 10 minutes, then store in a cool, dark place for up to 12 months. Once opened, refrigerate and use within 2 months.

BREAD & BUTTER CUCUMBER PICKLES

These are our signature pickles, the first ones we ever made, and now our bestsellers. They're a great way to start your pickling adventures. Small cucumbers are best for pickling, as their water content is lower: look out for bargain boxes of 'seconds' at farmers' markets – often the only difference is that they're not straight! Feel free to experiment with spices. These are classic pickle spices, but you could use whole chillies, garlic cloves, bay leaves and strips of lemon zest.

PREPARATION TIME
20 minutes, plus 1–2 hours salting

COOKING TIME
about 15 minutes, plus 10 minutes heat-processing

STORAGE
6–12 months

MAKES
about 6 x 375 ml (13 fl oz/1½ cup) jars

- 2 kg (4 lb 8 oz) Lebanese (short) cucumbers – the smaller, the better
- 2 tablespoons salt
- 1 litre (35 fl oz/4 cups) white wine vinegar
- 220 g (7¾ oz/1 cup) caster (superfine) sugar
- ½ teaspoon ground turmeric
- 2 small brown onions, thinly sliced
- 3 teaspoons brown mustard seeds
- 2 teaspoons fennel seeds
- 2 teaspoons dill seeds
- 2 teaspoons chilli flakes – optional
- 12–18 black peppercorns

Slice the cucumbers into rounds about the thickness of a coin. Put into a bowl and sprinkle with the salt, then leave to sit for an hour or two (or overnight). This is to draw out any excess liquid; the bigger the cucumbers, the longer it will take. Transfer to a large colander and leave to drain thoroughly.

Meanwhile, sterilise your jars (see page 250).

Make a brine by putting the vinegar, sugar, turmeric and 500 ml (17 fl oz/ 2 cups) of water into a medium non-reactive saucepan over low heat. Stir to dissolve the sugar, then increase the heat and bring to the boil. Let it bubble for 2–3 minutes, then remove from the heat.

Transfer the cucumbers to a large bowl. Add the onions, along with the mustard, fennel and dill seeds, and the chilli flakes, if using. Use your hands to mix everything together well.

When the jars are cool enough to handle, use small tongs or clean hands to carefully pack the cucumbers into the jars, adding 2 or 3 peppercorns to each jar. The jars should be full but not over-packed – the brine needs to cover every slice of cucumber, and if they are packed too tightly the brine won't be able to get into every nook and cranny (see page 252 for more on packing techniques).

Carefully fill the jars with the hot brine until the cucumbers are completely covered. Remove any air bubbles by gently tapping each jar on the work surface and sliding a butter knife or chopstick around the inside to release any hidden air pockets. You may need to add more brine or cucumbers after doing this (the liquid should reach about 1 cm/½ in from the top of the jar). Wipe the rims of the jars with a clean cloth or paper towel and seal.

Heat-process (see page 255) for 10 minutes, then store in a cool, dark place. Although these pickles will keep for up to 12 months, they start to lose their crunch after about 6 months.

PREPARATION TIME
30 minutes, plus
4 days fermenting

STORAGE
up to 6 months

MAKES
about 2 x 500 ml
(17 fl oz/2 cup) jars

FERMENTED PINEAPPLE & CHILLI SAMBAL

Jaimee started experimenting with fermented fruit last year. This fruit ferment comes from Sri Lanka, and it's sweet, spicy and salty. The pineapple, lime, coriander and ginger all retain their fresh flavour. We'd suggest serving it with seafood.

**2 kg (4 lb 8 oz) pineapple –
   about 2 medium-sized pineapples
large handful (1 cup, firmly packed) coriander
   (cilantro) leaves, chopped
2 teaspoons finely grated lime zest
1 tablespoon lime juice
1 tablespoon finely grated ginger
2 teaspoons chilli flakes or sliced fresh chilli
2 tablespoons salt**

Sterilise your jars (see page 250) and leave them to cool completely.

Peel the pineapples, then cut into 2 cm (¾ in) cubes, discarding the tough core. Place the pineapple in a non-reactive bowl, then add all the other ingredients. Using your hands, squish everything together and mix thoroughly.

Pack the pineapple mixture tightly into the jars (see page 252 for more on packing techniques), pressing down so that the juice rises above the pineapple and any air bubbles are released. Wipe the rims of the jars with a clean cloth or paper towel and seal.

Let the jars sit at room temperature (but out of direct sunlight) for 2–4 days. During this time, the lids will start to pop up, which is a sign of the fermenting process (see pages 256–259 for more details). Transfer the jars to the fridge and leave for a week before opening, then use within 6 months.

DILLY BEANS

These pickled beans are surprisingly delicious – and they get better with age, so although they're good to eat after a month or so, try to let them sit for as long as you can wait. The best ones we had sat for about 8 months before we opened them. Just remember that the spices will intensify over time, so go easy on the chilli if you're planning on letting them sit for a while. If you grow dill or fennel at home, let some go to seed and add the flowers too.

Serve these with cold meats, chopped through a salad, or eat straight out of the jar.

PREPARATION TIME
30 minutes

COOKING TIME
20 minutes, plus 15 minutes heat-processing

STORAGE
up to 2 years

MAKES
2–3 x 500 ml (17 fl oz/2 cup) jars

1 kg (2 lb 4 oz) hand-picked, good-quality green beans
1 litre (35 fl oz/4 cups) white wine vinegar
165 g (5¾ oz/¾ cup) caster (superfine) sugar
¼ teaspoon ground turmeric
1 teaspoon salt

FOR EACH JAR, YOU WILL NEED:
¼ teaspoon black peppercorns
½ teaspoon dill seeds
¼ teaspoon dried dill
1 small red chilli or garlic clove – optional
fennel flowers – optional

Wash the green beans and trim off any blemished ends. We like to leave the beans whole and with their stems intact, as it saves time and they look very pretty in the jar.

Sterilise your jars (see page 250).

Put the vinegar and 500 ml (17 fl oz/2 cups) of water in a medium non-reactive saucepan over low heat. Add the sugar, turmeric and salt and stir to dissolve, then increase the heat and bring to the boil. Let it bubble for 2–3 minutes, then remove from the heat.

When the jars are cool enough to handle, add the peppercorns, dill seeds, dried dill, chilli or garlic clove and fennel flowers, if using. Carefully pack the beans vertically in the jars (see page 252 for more on packing techniques), then pour in enough hot brine to completely cover the beans. Remove any air bubbles by gently tapping each jar on the work surface and sliding a butter knife or chopstick around the inside to release any hidden air pockets. You may need to add more brine or beans after doing this (the liquid should reach about 1 cm/½ in from the top of the jar). Wipe the rims of the jars with a clean cloth or paper towel and seal.

Heat-process (see page 255) for 15 minutes, then leave in a cool, dark place for a month before using. Unopened jars will last for up to 2 years; once opened, refrigerate and use within 3 months.

PREPARATION TIME
15 minutes

COOKING TIME
30 minutes, plus 15 minutes heat-processing – optional

STORAGE
1 week, or up to 6 months if heat-processed

MAKES
1.2 litres (42 fl oz) or 4 x 300 ml (10½ fl oz) jars

APRICOT & CARDAMOM COMPOTE

We make a lot of compotes at the picklery. They're a great way to use up excess fruit, especially quick-ripening ones, and they make good use of anything we have left over from our jam-making.

At the cafe, we started using them to make milkshakes (see below) as a kids' option, but they quickly found a following with adults too. Favourites have included mulberry (see page 63), rhubarb and rose, and salted prune. Although the crazy beetroot and chocolate version had some die-hard fans, we suspect it was often ordered with trepidation.

We usually have a jar of compote in the fridge at home to top muesli, porridge and ice cream, to use as a filling in sponge cakes, or to make ice blocks for the kids (see page 63).

1 kg (2 lb 4 oz) ripe, sweet apricots
20 cardamom pods
110 g (3¾ oz/½ cup) caster (superfine) sugar

Halve the apricots and discard the stones. Smash the cardamom pods with a pestle or the back of a wooden spoon, then tie in a muslin (cheesecloth) bag.

Put the apricots, sugar and the bag of cardamom pods into a medium non-reactive saucepan and add 350 ml (12 fl oz) of water. Cook over low heat and stir until the sugar dissolves. Simmer gently, with the lid on, for about 30 minutes, stirring occasionally. The final consistency is really up to you – we like to cook ours until the fruit is soft and almost falling apart, but still holds some shape.

Transfer to a container, keep in the fridge and use within a week. Or, for longer storage, bottle the compote. To do this, sterilise your jars (see page 250), then carefully fill the hot jars with the hot compote. Remove any air bubbles by gently tapping each jar on the work surface and sliding a butter knife or chopstick around the inside to release any hidden air pockets. Wipe the rims of the jars with a clean damp cloth and seal, then heat-process (see page 255) for 15 minutes. Unopened jars will keep in a cool, dark place for up to 6 months; once a jar is opened, the compote should be refrigerated and used within a week.

PREPARATION TIME
5 minutes

SERVES 2

APRICOT & CARDAMOM MILKSHAKE

400 ml (14 fl oz) milk
95 g (3¼ oz/⅓ cup) natural yoghurt
ice – optional
125 ml (4 fl oz/½ cup) apricot and cardamom compote (see above)
honey, to taste

Place all the ingredients in a food processor or blender and blitz until smooth. Add honey to taste, then blend again. Pour into two chilled glasses and serve.

HAZELNUT MERINGUE CAKE WITH LIME CURD, PEACH & MANGO

One of our original chefs, Steph, would make show-stopper cakes on special occasions. Here she's shared one of her favourites, which makes the most of seasonal fruit. You'll need to make the lime curd the day before; any left-over curd will keep for a few days in the fridge.

PREPARATION TIME
50 minutes, plus overnight chilling

COOKING TIME
1¼ hours

MAKES
1 x 20 cm (8 in) cake

- 6–8 yellow or doughnut peaches, very thinly sliced
- 2 mangoes, thinly sliced
- 75 g (2¾ oz/½ cup) toasted hazelnuts, skinned and roughly chopped
- a few small mint leaves and fine strips of lime zest, to garnish

LIME CURD
- 12 g (⅓ oz) powdered gelatine
- finely grated zest and juice of 12 limes
- 300 g (10½ oz) caster (superfine) sugar
- 12 free-range eggs
- 330 g (11½ oz) chilled unsalted butter, diced

HAZELNUT MERINGUE
- vegetable oil spray
- 9 free-range egg whites
- 335 g (11¾ oz) caster (superfine) sugar
- 520 g (1 lb 2½ oz/4¾ cups) hazelnut meal
- ½ teaspoon salt
- 2 vanilla beans, split and seeds scraped

For the lime curd, mix the gelatine with 125 ml (4 fl oz/½ cup) of water, then set aside. Put the lime zest and juice in a saucepan, then whisk in the sugar and eggs. Place over low heat and very slowly bring to the boil, stirring constantly so the eggs don't scramble. Pour into a food processor or blender, add the gelatine mixture and butter and whiz until the butter has melted and the curd is smooth. Pour into a large shallow container and leave to set in the fridge overnight.

The next day, for the hazelnut meringue, preheat the oven to 150°C (300°F/gas mark 2). Line three baking trays with baking paper and draw a 20 cm (8 in) circle on each one. Spray very lightly with vegetable oil.

Using an electric mixer, beat the egg whites until soft peaks form. Gradually add the sugar and keep whisking until stiff and glossy. Gently fold in the hazelnut meal, salt and vanilla seeds until just incorporated.

Divide the mixture evenly between the circles, spreading it out to the edges. Bake for 60 minutes or until set and dry, then remove from the oven and leave to cool completely.

To assemble, fill a piping bag with the lime curd. Place one of the meringues on a serving plate and pipe curd evenly over it, in circles, then top with a third of the peach and mango slices. Repeat these layers twice more, then sprinkle over the hazelnuts and garnish with the mint leaves and lime zest.

AUTUMN

PREPARATION TIME
25 minutes,
plus overnight
macerating

COOKING TIME
30 minutes

STORAGE
up to 12 months

MAKES
about 2 x 400 ml
(14 fl oz) jars

BLACKBERRY JAM

This jam is so good that we have to hide the jar at the back of the fridge so it doesn't get demolished in one sitting. Don't cook the jam for too long – it sets surprisingly quickly.

If you're lucky enough to get your hands on some home-grown blackberries, make this jam! Or you could try making it with mulberries; just make sure you hull them before you start.

1 kg (2 lb 4 oz) blackberries, stems removed, rinsed
750 g (1 lb 10 oz) caster (superfine) sugar
125 ml (4 fl oz/½ cup) lemon juice
1 tablespoon finely grated lemon zest
   (from 1 or 2 lemons)

Put the blackberries into a bowl with the sugar and mix gently. Cover the bowl with plastic wrap or a plate and leave to sit overnight in the fridge.

The next day, lightly squash the berries with your hands or a potato masher, then transfer to a medium sized non-reactive saucepan. Place over low heat, add the lemon juice and zest, and stir until the sugar has dissolved. Turn the heat up to medium–high and boil the jam rapidly until setting point is reached (see page 250), stirring occasionally to avoid burning. This jam is quick to cook, approximately 20–30 minutes, and it tends to set quite firmly, so be careful not to overcook it. A tasty, runny blackberry jam is much more delicious than an overcooked and hard-set one.

Meanwhile, sterilise your jars (see page 250). Carefully pour the hot jam into the hot jars and seal immediately. Store the jam in a cool, dark place for up to 12 months. Once opened, refrigerate and use within a month – though it never lasts that long in our house.

BITTER LIME MARMALADE

After many happy years of marmalade-making, this is a firm favourite. A beautiful marmalade with thin strips of rind and ginger in a pretty, clear gel, it's incredibly juicy and full of flavour, but has a nice bitter edge that stops it from being too sweet. You can also make this with grapefruit, lemons, oranges or a mixture of citrus fruit. Try adding other flavours too, like juniper with grapefruit, or cloves with oranges.

PREPARATION TIME
30 minutes

COOKING TIME
2 hours

STORAGE
up to 2 years

MAKES
about 6 x 300 ml (10½ fl oz) jars

1 kg (2 lb 4 oz) limes
150–300 g (5½ oz–10½ oz) ginger, depending on how strong you like it, peeled and thinly sliced into matchsticks – optional
1.5 kg (3 lb 5 oz) caster (superfine) sugar

Juice all the limes. After juicing, flatten each lime half on the bench with the palm of your hand and then slice as thinly as possible into matchsticks.

Put the lime matchsticks and juice into a jam pan or large wide saucepan, then add 3 litres (105 fl oz/12 cups) of water and the ginger, if using. Bring to the boil, then simmer over low heat for about 1–1½ hours, or until the lime rind is soft and translucent.

Turn off the heat and slowly add the sugar, stirring until it has dissolved. Bring the marmalade back to the boil over medium heat, then boil steadily, stirring every now and then, for about 20 minutes or until it reaches setting point (see page 250). Let the marmalade sit for 5 minutes or so.

Meanwhile, sterilise your jars (see page 250). Carefully fill the hot jars with the hot jam. Remove any air bubbles by gently tapping each jar on the work surface and sliding a butter knife or chopstick around the inside to release any hidden air pockets. Wipe the rims of the jars with a clean damp cloth and seal. Store in a cool, dark place for up to 2 years; once opened, refrigerate and use within 6 months.

PREPARATION TIME
30 minutes

COOKING TIME
1¾ hours

STORAGE
up to 2 years

MAKES
6–8 x 300 ml
(10½ fl oz) jars

QUINCE & APPLE JAM

These two autumn fruits make a beautifully rich jam. Watch as the quince magically transforms to a deep red colour as it cooks. You can add spices too, if you like – cloves, cinnamon or allspice go very well with this combination.

juice of 4 lemons
1 kg (2 lb 4 oz) apples
1.5 kg (3 lb 5 oz) quinces
5 cloves – optional
finely grated zest of 1 lemon
2 kg (4 lb 8 oz) caster (superfine) sugar

Fill a large bowl with water and add the juice of one of the lemons. (This is to put the cut apples and quinces into to stop them from going brown while you're preparing them.)

Peel and core the apples, then cut them into 2 cm (¾ in) cubes, dropping them into the bowl of water and lemon juice as you go. Peel and core the quinces and cut into 2 cm (¾ in) cubes as well, adding them to the bowl with the apples.

Drain the quinces and apples and put into a jam pan or large wide saucepan with the cloves, if using, and 3 litres (105 fl oz/12 cups) of water. Place over low heat and simmer slowly until the apples and quinces are soft and starting to break down – this can take up to 1 hour.

Add the lemon zest, the remaining lemon juice and the sugar to the fruit and stir until the sugar has dissolved. Turn up the heat and boil the jam rapidly, stirring often to stop it catching, until setting point is reached (see page 250), about 30–40 minutes. Helpfully, this jam also turns a rich pinky red when it is ready.

Meanwhile, sterilise your jars (see page 250).

Carefully pour the hot jam into the hot jars. Wipe the rims of the jars with a clean damp cloth or paper towel and put the lids on. Store in a cool, dark place for up to 2 years. Once opened, refrigerate and use within a few months.

WATERCRESS & NASTURTIUM BUTTER WITH RADISHES

PREPARATION TIME
15 minutes

SERVES
4–6 as a starter or snack

This is our take on the classic way of serving radishes with butter and salt. Nasturtiums grow plentifully in our suburb, and are in season in autumn. They are one of the most common backyard trading products our customers bring in, so we use them a lot on our menu. Their strong peppery flavour is nice in small amounts, but be careful not to over-do it. Nasturtiums belong to the cress family, so if you don't have any, just use the watercress.

This recipe makes more flavoured butter than you need here, as it's hard to successfully make a smaller amount in the food processor, but the rest can be stored, well wrapped, in the fridge or freezer. Use it on a ploughman's plate (see page 160), slip some under the skin of a chicken before roasting or add a slice to a freshly grilled steak.

250 g (9 oz) unsalted butter, softened
200 g (7 oz/1 bunch) watercress, washed and thoroughly dried, coarse stems removed
large handful (1 cup, firmly packed) nasturtium leaves, roughly chopped
1 shallot, finely chopped
finely grated zest of ½ lemon
500 g (1 lb 2 oz/2 bunches) radishes

Put all the ingredients except the radishes into a food processor, then add a couple of pinches of salt and pulse until smooth, stopping every now and then to scrape down the sides with a rubber spatula. Weigh out 80 g (2¾ oz) of the butter and place on a serving plate or press into a small bowl.

Place the rest of the butter on a rectangular piece of baking paper and shape into a log. Firmly roll up the butter in the baking paper, pressing it into a cylindrical shape as you go – it should be firm and tight. Wrap in plastic wrap and store in the fridge for up to 10 days, or in the freezer for up to 3 months.

Cut the radishes in half and place on a plate. Serve with the soft butter and some more salt.

PREPARATION TIME
15 minutes

COOKING TIME
45 minutes, plus
10 minutes resting

SERVES 4

LEEK, APPLE & GOAT'S CURD FRITTATA

Frittatas often get a bad rap, but made with good eggs and seasonal produce, they're a revelation. With a balance of sweet, oniony flavours from the leeks, acidity from the apple and nuttiness from the pumpkin seeds, this is a delicate frittata that's delicious served with a leafy salad or a slice of bread.

500 g (1 lb 2 oz) leeks, ends trimmed
2½ tablespoons olive oil, plus extra for drizzling
2 garlic cloves, finely chopped
1 apple, ideally pink lady, coarsely grated
1 tablespoon chopped parsley, plus extra to serve
1 teaspoon chopped thyme, plus extra to serve
pinch of freshly grated nutmeg
6 free-range eggs, lightly beaten
100 g (3½ oz) goat's curd, other fresh curd or quark
1 tablespoon pumpkin seeds, toasted

Preheat the oven to 140°C (275°F/gas mark 1).

Wash the leeks thoroughly, then slice both green and white parts into thin rings. Heat 1½ tablespoons of the olive oil in a medium saucepan and sauté the leeks and garlic over medium heat until they soften. Season with salt and pepper, then stir in the apple, parsley, thyme and nutmeg.

Place a 20 cm (8 in) ovenproof frying pan over medium heat and pour in the remaining tablespoon of oil (you want a thin film of oil over the base and sides of the pan – add a little more if needed). Add the leek and apple mixture, spreading it out over the base of the pan, then pour over the beaten egg. Add dollops of curd to the frittata and sprinkle over the pumpkin seeds, then transfer to the oven and bake for 35–40 minutes or until just set.

Leave the frittata to sit for about 10 minutes, then serve drizzled with a little more olive oil and garnished with some extra chopped thyme and parsley.

KALE, APPLE, SPROUTS & SEED SALAD WITH BUTTERMILK DRESSING

PREPARATION TIME
25 minutes

SERVES 4

This recipe from the cafe is typical of our approach to salads: matching seeds, nuts and herbs with light dressings and beautiful produce – in this case, sprouts grown by Amanda, our veggie supplier's wife (see page 261 for more on sprouting).

Kale gets tougher as it gets bigger, so try to get your hands on smaller leaves for this raw salad: either pick it young or choose carefully at your greengrocer. If you can only get larger coarser kale, slice it very thinly or substitute cavolo nero. You need genuine buttermilk for this dressing. A by-product in the making of cultured butter, it's tangy and full of live cultures, and is a world away from the commercially produced buttermilk you find in the supermarket. If you can't get your hands on good buttermilk, you'd be better off using kefir or yoghurt.

- 8–12 green or purple kale leaves, depending on size
- 2 large handfuls mixed herb sprigs, such as flat-leaf parsley, mint and dill
- 1 red apple, thinly sliced
- ½ red onion, thinly sliced
- 100 g (3½ oz/1 cup) lentil or bean sprouts (see page 261)
- 4 tablespoons mixed pumpkin and sunflower seeds, toasted

BUTTERMILK DRESSING
- 100 ml (3½ fl oz) buttermilk
- 2 tablespoons apple balsamic vinegar or cider vinegar
- 2 teaspoons honey
- 2 teaspoons Cornersmith mustard (see page 159) or other grainy mustard
- 100 ml (3½ fl oz) vegetable oil
- 100 ml (3½ fl oz) olive oil

For the dressing, whisk together the buttermilk, vinegar, honey and mustard in a bowl. Season with salt and pepper, then add the oils in a slow steady stream, whisking constantly to emulsify. For a silky texture, blitz with a stick blender.

To prepare the kale, strip the leaves from the stems, then thinly slice the stems and tear the leaves into bite-sized pieces. Pick the herb leaves and tear into smaller pieces.

In a large bowl, combine the kale leaves and stems with the herbs, apple, onion, sprouts and three-quarters of the seeds. Season with salt and pepper, then add the dressing and toss gently.

Place the salad in a serving bowl or on plates and scatter over the remaining toasted seeds to serve.

PREPARATION TIME
25 minutes

COOKING TIME
10 minutes

SERVES 4

BITTERSWEET TABOULEH WITH RADICCHIO & POMEGRANATE

Here is Sabine's autumn adaptation of the classic Middle Eastern dish, using buckwheat for a gluten-free tabouleh. The bitterness of the radicchio beautifully balances the acidity of the tomatoes and pomegranate and the sweetness of the pomegranate syrup. Add a dollop of yoghurt just before serving, if you like.

100 g (3½ oz) buckwheat
1 Lebanese (short) cucumber, finely diced
2 ox-heart tomatoes, finely chopped
½ small radicchio, finely shredded
seeds from 1 smallish pomegranate
finely grated zest and juice of 1–2 lemons
2 handfuls roughly chopped or torn mixed herbs, such as parsley, mint and dill
80 ml (2½ fl oz/⅓ cup) olive oil
2–3 pinches sumac
1 tablespoon pomegranate syrup (see page 142) or pomegranate molasses

Put the buckwheat into a large saucepan of salted boiling water. As soon as the water comes back up to the boil, reduce the heat and simmer for 6–8 minutes. When the buckwheat is done, the grains should still have a slight bite to them. Drain and leave to cool.

Mix the buckwheat, cucumber, tomatoes, radicchio and pomegranate seeds in a bowl. Add the lemon zest and juice, three-quarters of the herbs and season with salt and pepper, then gently toss everything together.

To serve, place the tabouleh in a large bowl, then pour over the olive oil. Scatter over the sumac and the rest of the herbs and drizzle over the pomegranate syrup.

CITRUS-BRAISED FENNEL

Make this one! The pairing of fennel and citrus is amazing – and, happily, both are around during autumn and into winter. Sprinkled with fetta cheese and served with some cooked grains or bread, this dish makes a delicious vegetarian meal, and is also the perfect side dish for roast chicken or pork.

PREPARATION TIME
15 minutes

COOKING TIME
40 minutes

SERVES 4

3 medium fennel bulbs
3 tablespoons olive oil
125 ml (4 fl oz/½ cup) apple cider
juice and finely grated zest of 1 lemon
juice and finely grated zest of 1 orange
2 thyme sprigs
1 bay leaf
3 garlic cloves, peeled and crushed
   with the back of a knife
1 teaspoon chopped parsley
1 teaspoon chopped fennel fronds

Wash the fennel bulbs and trim off any green feathery fronds, reserving them for later. Cut the bulbs lengthways into slices about 1 cm (½ in) thick, leaving in the core, so the slices don't fall apart – the fennel will become amazingly soft and delicious after the braising.

Choose a wide, lidded saucepan that will hold all the fennel in a single layer. Pour in 2 tablespoons of the olive oil and place over medium–high heat. Add the fennel slices, season with salt and pepper, and cook for 2–3 minutes on each side or until golden brown.

Add the cider, lemon juice and orange juice and reduce until almost all the liquid has evaporated. Add the citrus zests, thyme, bay leaf and garlic, then pour in enough water to just cover the fennel. Bring to the boil, then reduce the heat to a slow simmer and add the remaining tablespoon of olive oil. Cover with a circle of baking paper, pressing it directly onto the fennel, then put the lid on the saucepan and braise for 20–25 minutes or until the fennel is soft. By the time the fennel is ready, the liquid should have reduced to a sauce.

Serve the fennel on a platter or large plate, drizzled with the sauce and scattered with the chopped parsley and fennel fronds.

PREPARATION TIME
45 minutes

COOKING TIME
20 minutes,
plus 15 minutes
heat-processing

STORAGE
3 months, or up to
12 months if heat-
processed

MAKES
1 x 300 ml
(10½ fl oz) bottle

POMEGRANATE SYRUP

Making this may seem quite labour intensive, but it really is worth the effort to capture the pomegranate flavour for the rest of the year, especially as their season is so short. Very versatile, this sweet, sour and slightly tannic syrup works well in both savoury and sweet dishes: try it on top of yoghurt, with meats (see page 86) or in marinades and dressings.

10–12 pomegranates
2 tablespoons caster (superfine) sugar

First you need to extract the seeds from the pomegranates, taking care to discard all the bitter white pith. An easy way to do this is to bash all over the outside of each pomegranate with a wooden spoon. Cut the pomegranate in half over a bowl and lots of the seeds will fall out. Continue bashing the outside of the pomegranate to loosen more seeds, then use your fingers to pick out any remaining seeds.

Juice the pomegranate seeds in a juicer. If you don't have a juicer, blitz them in a food processor, then strain the juice through a fine sieve. You need 500 ml (17 fl oz/2 cups) of juice.

Put the juice and sugar into a non-reactive saucepan. Place over low heat and slowly bring to a simmer, stirring every now and then. Let it simmer for 15–20 minutes or until it thickens slightly, but isn't too syrupy.

Meanwhile, sterilise your bottle (see page 250).

Let the syrup sit for a few minutes, then skim off any scum before carefully pouring the hot syrup into the hot bottle. Wipe the rim of the bottle with a clean cloth or paper towel, then seal. Either heat-process (see page 255) for 15 minutes for longer storage, or refrigerate and use within 3 months.

PICKLED SARDINES

Thanks to Sabine's European background, we serve lots of pickled and smoked fish. First the fish is steeped in brine to break it down, then it's pickled to preserve it. Oily fish such as herring and sardines really benefit from this treatment, as the vinegar in the pickling liquid helps to cut through the richness of the fish. These sardines can be served on toast or with any salad in this book. If you get a taste for them, it's worth making a bigger quantity, as they'll keep for up to a month in the fridge; just pack the brined sardines in layers with the onion, lemon and spices in sterilised jars (see page 250). Both the brine and the pickling liquid can be made ahead of time.

PREPARATION TIME
30 minutes, plus 1–2 days brining and pickling

SERVES 4

35 g (1¼ oz/¼ cup) salt
500 g (1 lb 2 oz) butterflied sardines (about 8 small ones)
1 red onion, thinly sliced
1 lemon, thinly sliced

PICKLING LIQUID
500 ml (17 fl oz/2 cups) white wine vinegar
55 g (2 oz/¼ cup) caster (superfine) sugar
1 teaspoon mustard seeds
2 teaspoons allspice berries
2 teaspoons black peppercorns
1 teaspoon dill seeds
3 bay leaves
3 cloves

Put the salt and 1 litre (35 fl oz/4 cups) of water in a non-reactive saucepan and heat just enough to dissolve the salt. Leave to cool completely, then immerse the sardines in this brine and refrigerate for at least 8 hours, or up to 24 hours.

For the pickling liquid, put all the ingredients into a non-reactive saucepan with 250 ml (9 fl oz/1 cup) of water. Bring to the boil, stirring every now and then so the sugar dissolves evenly. Let it bubble for 2 minutes, then remove from the heat and leave to cool completely.

Take the sardines out of the brine and pat dry with paper towel. Place the sardines in a non-reactive container, layering them with the onion and lemon slices. Pour over the pickling liquid, then refrigerate for at least a day before using. Drain before serving.

PREPARATION TIME
20 minutes, plus
30 minutes marinating

COOKING TIME
30 minutes

SERVES 4

POTATO SALAD

This potato salad uses all the elements we have on hand to make a light and bright salad: our Cornersmith mustard (see page 159) and pickles, plus left-over pickling liquid for the dressing. If you find you don't have quite enough pickling liquid, you can top up to the required amount with a good-quality white wine vinegar. For a heartier version of this salad, add some pan-fried speck or bacon and mix a little mayo into the dressing.

1 kg (2 lb 4 oz) boiling potatoes, such as
    dutch cream or nicola, scrubbed
2–4 shallots, thinly sliced
270 ml (9½ fl oz) pickling liquid from the pickles
    (see below)
145 ml (4¾ fl oz) olive oil
2 teaspoons dijon mustard
2 large handfuls mixed herb sprigs,
    such as dill, tarragon and parsley
4–6 radishes, very thinly sliced
130 g (4½ oz/1 cup) drained bread and butter
    cucumber pickles (see page 111), or other pickles
1–2 Lebanese (short) cucumbers, thinly sliced

Put the unpeeled potatoes in a saucepan and cover with salted cold water. Cover with a lid, bring to the boil and simmer for 25–30 minutes until tender. Drain well, then leave to cool. (This can be done the day before, if you like.)

Thickly slice the potatoes and mix with the shallots. Bring 200 ml (7 fl oz) of the pickling liquid to the boil in a small saucepan, then pour over the potatoes and shallots. Season with salt and pepper, drizzle with a tablespoon of the olive oil and mix well. Leave to marinate for at least 30 minutes, or overnight in the fridge if that's more convenient.

For the dressing, combine the remaining pickling liquid and olive oil with the mustard in a screw-top jar. Season with salt and pepper, then put the lid on the jar and shake well to emulsify.

Tear the herbs into smaller pieces and put into a large bowl. Add the potato mixture, radishes, pickles and fresh cucumber. Pour over the dressing and gently toss everything to combine.

Place the salad in a serving bowl or on plates and serve straightaway.

JAIMEE'S SAUERKRAUT

Here's another recipe from Cornersmith's fermenter Jaimee (see pages 256–259 for her tips and advice). She describes sauerkraut as the queen of fermented vegetables, and this is her all-time favourite recipe. Across Europe and all over Asia, some kind of pickled cabbage is an essential condiment on the table. This recipe has classic Eastern European flavours, and is excellent with meat, potatoes, or on a Reuben sandwich (see page 210).

PREPARATION TIME
45 minutes, plus 2 days fermenting

STORAGE
up to 6 months

MAKES
2 x 750 ml
(26 fl oz/3 cup) jars

1 small red cabbage (about 1.2 kg/2 lb 10 oz)
1 small white cabbage (about 1.2 kg/2 lb 10 oz)
3 tablespoons salt
1 tablespoon caraway seeds
½ teaspoon juniper berries

Sterilise your jars (see page 250) and leave them to cool completely.

Discard the outer leaves of the cabbages. Cut each cabbage in half and cut out the core, then shred finely.

Put the shredded cabbage in a large bowl with the salt, caraway seeds and juniper berries, then pound with a wooden mallet or meat hammer for about 10 minutes, or until the juices are released.

Pack the cabbage tightly into the jars, pressing down so that the liquid rises above the cabbage and any air bubbles are released. Keep going until the jars are full and the liquid covers the cabbage by about 2 cm (¾ in) – if there's not enough liquid, top up the jars with filtered or bottled water. Wipe the rims of the jars with a clean cloth or paper towel and seal.

Let the jars sit at room temperature (but out of direct sunlight) for 2–4 days. During this time, the lids will start to pop up, which is a sign of the fermenting process (see page 259 for more details). Transfer the jars of sauerkraut to the fridge and leave for a week before opening, then use within 6 months.

PREPARATION TIME
20 minutes

COOKING TIME
50–60 minutes, plus 15 minutes heat-processing

STORAGE
up to 6 months

MAKES
4 x 300 ml (10½ fl oz) jars

APPLE SAUCE WITH CIDER

For this variation on apple sauce, we add locally made cloudy cider to make the sauce rich enough to accompany meaty dishes. It's important to include apple varieties with a high level of acidity, such as granny smith or pink lady, or it will be too sweet. For an extra layer of flavour, stir some finely chopped sage through the sauce just before serving.

If you don't want to make a batch of this for the pantry, you could halve the recipe and just serve the apple sauce as soon as it's ready, rather than bottling and heat-processing it. Any leftovers will keep for a few days in the fridge.

1 kg (2 lb 4 oz) granny smith apples
1 kg (2 lb 4 oz) gala apples
juice of 1 lemon
80 g (2¾ oz) brown sugar
1 bay leaf
500 ml (17 fl oz/2 cups) cider
pinch of freshly grated nutmeg

Peel, core and quarter the apples, dropping them into a large bowl full of cold water with a squeeze of lemon juice added as you go, to stop them going brown.

Drain the apples and put them in a large saucepan with the sugar, bay leaf and cider. Cover and cook over medium heat for 30–40 minutes, or until the apples start to soften and fall apart. Take off the lid and simmer for 5–10 minutes or until almost all the liquid has evaporated.

Meanwhile, sterilise your jars (see page 250).

Remove the pan from the heat, replace the lid and leave to sit for 10 minutes, then lightly mash the apples with a whisk. This will give you a rather chunky, rustic sauce; if you prefer your apple sauce smooth, blitz it with a stick blender. Stir in the nutmeg, then taste the sauce for seasoning and sharpen with a little lemon juice, if necessary.

Carefully ladle the hot apple sauce into the hot jars. Wipe the rims of the jars with a clean cloth or paper towel and seal immediately, then heat-process (see page 255) for 15 minutes.

The apple sauce can be used straightaway, but will keep in a cool, dark place for up to 6 months. Once a jar is opened, refrigerate and use within 3–4 days.

ROASTED EGGPLANT & RICOTTA WITH WALNUTS & POMEGRANATE

This dish combines everything that's at its best in autumn: eggplants, walnuts and pomegranate. Serve it as a dip to start an autumn dinner, or spread on bread for lunch. The eggplants can be roasted and drained the day before to make things easier.

PREPARATION TIME
15 minutes

COOKING TIME
45–60 minutes, plus 1–2 hours draining

SERVES 4

1 kg (2 lb 4 oz) eggplants (aubergines)
handful (½ cup) parsley leaves
handful (½ cup) mint leaves
100 g (3½ oz) ricotta
juice of 1 lemon
55 g (2 oz) walnuts, ideally new-season ones, toasted and roughly chopped
1 teaspoon olive oil
1 teaspoon pomegranate syrup (see page 142) or pomegranate molasses

Preheat the oven to 200°C (400°F/gas mark 6).

Prick the eggplants all over with a fork or skewer. Place on a baking tray and roast for 45–60 minutes, or until they totally collapse – they will look really ugly and burnt, but don't worry, that's what you want.

When the eggplants are cool enough to handle, cut them open lengthways and scrape out the flesh with a spoon. Put the eggplant flesh into a colander and leave to drain for 1–2 hours; longer is better, but if you're pushed for time you can speed up the process by sitting a plate with a tin of food (or jar of pickles) on top of the eggplant in the colander.

Tear about three-quarters of the parsley and mint leaves into smaller pieces. Transfer the drained eggplant flesh to a bowl and break it apart with a fork, then gently fold through the ricotta, lemon juice, walnuts and the torn herbs. Season to taste with salt and pepper.

Place in a serving bowl, then drizzle with the olive oil and pomegranate syrup and scatter over the rest of the herbs.

PREPARATION TIME
20 minutes, plus
8–10 hours cooling
and brining

COOKING TIME
30 minutes, plus
15 minutes resting

SERVES 4

PORK CHOPS WITH FENNEL, APPLE SAUCE & MUSTARD

With a well-stocked fridge and pantry, you can have this autumnal meal on the table in no time – just remember to make the brine in advance so it has plenty of time to cool, and allow an hour or two to brine the chops. Brining meat before cooking tenderises and seasons it beautifully.

4 x 200 g (7 oz) pasture-raised pork chops
2 tablespoons grapeseed oil
1 quantity citrus-braised fennel (see page 141)
6 tablespoons apple sauce with cider (see page 150)
4 tablespoons Cornersmith mustard (see page 159)
   or other grainy mustard

BRINE
100 g (3½ oz) salt
100 g (3½ oz) brown sugar
1 teaspoon juniper berries
1 teaspoon black peppercorns
1 bay leaf
1 clove
2 allspice berries
½ teaspoon yellow mustard seeds

To make the brine, combine all the ingredients with 1 litre (35 fl oz/4 cups) of water in a large saucepan. Place over low heat and stir until the salt and sugar have dissolved, then increase the heat and bring to the boil. Let the brine bubble away for 2 minutes, then remove from the heat and leave to cool for 6–8 hours.

Lay the pork chops in a single layer in a shallow non-reactive dish and pour over the cooled brine. Refrigerate for 1½ hours.

Remove the chops from the brine and dry thoroughly with paper towel. Season very lightly with salt and pepper – remember the meat will already have absorbed some salt from the brine.

Preheat the oven to 160°C (315°F/gas mark 2–3). Heat the oil in a large ovenproof frying pan over medium heat – make sure the heat isn't too high, or the sugar from the brine will burn. Add the chops and cook for 5–6 minutes each side, or until golden brown. Transfer to the oven and cook for 3–5 minutes, then remove from the oven and leave to rest for 12–15 minutes.

Serve the chops on individual plates with the fennel, apple sauce and mustard on the side.

CORNERSMITH MUSTARD

Ever since we started making our own mustard at Cornersmith, production hasn't stopped! As well as selling lots in our shop at the picklery, we use it in all sorts of dishes in the cafe, including our take on a Reuben sandwich (see page 210), our ploughman's plate (see page 160) and with pork chops (see page 156).

We tweak our mustard according to the time of year, using sage in autumn, horseradish or rosemary in winter, and thyme in spring. Mustard is such a great food to make from scratch, with lots of opportunities to experiment with different flavours, so feel free to try using other herbs, or to add freshly chopped herbs when serving. A jar of homemade mustard also makes an impressive gift.

PREPARATION TIME
15 minutes, plus 3–4 weeks maturing

STORAGE
3 months, or up to 2 years if heat-processed

MAKES
4 x 300 ml (10½ fl oz) jars

210 g (7½ oz) yellow mustard seeds
210 g (7½ oz) brown mustard seeds
160 ml (5¼ fl oz) boiling water
40 g (1½ oz) fine salt
125 g (4½ oz) honey
470 ml (16½ fl oz) cider vinegar
1 tablespoon chopped sage

Grind two-thirds of the mustard seeds into a fine powder using a spice grinder or clean coffee grinder – you'll probably need to do this in a few batches. Tip the mustard powder into a large bowl, then add the rest of the mustard seeds and the boiling water. Leave to sit for 5 minutes.

Mix the salt and honey into the vinegar until well combined, then whisk into the mustard mixture. Transfer the mustard to a non-reactive container and leave in the fridge to mature for 3–4 weeks.

Fold in the chopped sage before packing the mustard into cool sterilised jars (see page 250). Store jars in a cool, dark place for up to 3 months. For longer storage, heat-process (see page 255) for 15 minutes, then store for up to 2 years. Refrigerate after opening.

PREPARATION TIME
15 minutes

SERVES 4

PLOUGHMAN'S PLATE

Reflecting Alex's affinity with English-style larder food, this is our most popular lunchtime dish at Cornersmith. We use our ploughman's plate as an excuse to showcase the best of the season's fresh produce alongside our favourite pickles and preserves. Feel free to do the same and use whatever you have or what looks good at the market.

8–10 radishes, cut in half if large
2 apples, halved, or a bunch of grapes
8 slices cheddar
8 slices pasture-raised ham
1 tablespoon Cornersmith mustard (see page 159) or other grainy mustard
40 g (1½ oz) cultured butter
pickles, such as bread and butter cucumber (see page 111), and/or chutney, such as pear, lemon and rosemary (see page 163)
8 slices sourdough bread

Arrange all the ingredients except the bread on a wooden platter.

Serve with fresh or lightly toasted sourdough.

PEAR, LEMON & ROSEMARY CHUTNEY

A versatile chutney that is equally at home with meats or in a sandwich as it is on a ploughman's plate (see page 160). You need pears that are full of flavour and on the riper side for this. We don't usually peel the fruit for this country-style chutney, as we like it to retain some texture, but if you want a smoother consistency, peel the pears and cut them into smaller chunks.

We've suggested red wine vinegar here for a richer, more wintry feel, but apple cider vinegar also works, as does a mix of pears and apples.

PREPARATION TIME
45 minutes

COOKING TIME
2 hours

STORAGE
up to 12 months

MAKES
5 x 300 ml
(10½ fl oz) jars

80 ml (2½ fl oz/⅓ cup) vegetable oil
500 g (1 lb 2 oz) onions, thinly sliced
2 kg (4 lb 8 oz) ripe pears, cut into 2 cm (¾ in) cubes
2 teaspoons salt
1 teaspoon freshly ground black pepper
4 cloves
finely grated zest of 1 lemon
1 rosemary sprig, leaves picked and finely chopped
600 ml (21 fl oz) red wine vinegar
250 g (9 oz) caster (superfine) sugar

Heat the vegetable oil in a large heavy-based saucepan over low–medium heat. Sauté the onions until soft but not browned. Stir in the pear, salt, pepper and cloves, along with half of the lemon zest and half of the rosemary, and cook until the pears soften slightly.

Add the vinegar and sugar. Stir until the sugar has dissolved, then increase the heat to medium. Cook the chutney, stirring regularly to stop it sticking, for a good hour or so, until the desired consistency is reached: the chutney should be glossy and thick, with no puddles of liquid on the surface. Stir through the rest of the rosemary and cook for another 5 minutes. Taste and add more lemon zest or salt, if needed, then set aside to cool for 10 minutes.

Meanwhile, sterilise your jars (see page 250).

Carefully ladle the hot chutney into the hot jars. Wipe the rims of the jars with a clean cloth or paper towel and seal immediately.

Leave the chutney to sit for at least 6 weeks before using. Unopened jars will keep for 12 months in a cool, dark place; once opened, store in the fridge and use within 3 months.

PREPARATION TIME
25 minutes

COOKING TIME
10 minutes,
plus 10 minutes
heat-processing

STORAGE
up to 12 months

MAKES
2–3 × 500 ml
(17 fl oz/2 cup) jars

PICKLED RED GRAPES

It might be more unusual to see fruit instead of vegetables in a pickling liquid, but we pickle lots of fruit and find the vinegar offsets its sweetness beautifully. These pickled grapes go well with soft cheese – try them on top of baked ricotta (see page 233) – and they make an interesting addition to a salad (see page 217) or roasted meat dishes (just add them to the roasting tin about 5 minutes before the end of the cooking time). Other fruit that can be successfully pickled include quinces, pears, plums or sugar plums, rhubarb and cumquats (see page 234).

500 ml (17 fl oz/2 cups) red wine vinegar
440 g (15½ oz/2 cups) caster (superfine) sugar
6 allspice berries
12 black peppercorns
3 slices ginger
1 kg (2 lb 4 oz) red grapes

First sterilise your jars (see page 250).

Make a brine by putting the vinegar, sugar and 500 ml (17 fl oz/2 cups) of water in a small non-reactive saucepan over low heat. Stir until the sugar has dissolved, then increase the heat and bring to the boil. Take off the heat.

When the jars are cool enough to handle, put 2 allspice berries, 4 peppercorns and a slice of ginger into each one. Carefully pack in the grapes (see page 252 for packing techniques), then let them soften in the hot brine for a few minutes; they will shrink and you may be able to pack in some more. Remove any air bubbles by gently tapping each jar on the work surface and sliding a butter knife or chopstick around the inside to release any hidden air pockets. You may need to add more grapes or brine after doing this (the liquid should reach about 1 cm/½ in from the top of the jar). Wipe the rims of the jars with a clean cloth and seal, then heat-process (see page 255) for 15 minutes.

Store in a cool, dark place for at least a month before using. Unopened jars will keep for up to 12 months; once opened, refrigerate and use within 3 months.

CORN SALSA

The corn season spans the end of summer and the start of autumn, and we often bottle this towards the end of the season. It complements any Mexican-style meal, but is also good with scrambled, poached or fried eggs, or on a chicken or ham sandwich. Try mixing some corn salsa through a bread dough for a simple corn bread, or stir a couple of spoonfuls into a firm pancake batter to make quick corn fritters.

PREPARATION TIME
15 minutes

COOKING TIME
30 minutes, plus 10 minutes heat-processing – optional

STORAGE
1 month, or up to 12 months if heat-processed

MAKES
about 4 x 300 ml (10½ fl oz) jars

1½ tablespoons vegetable oil
1 large onion, finely chopped
1 tablespoon salt
2 small red capsicums (peppers), diced
5 small corn cobs, kernels cut from cobs
½ teaspoon ground coriander
¼ teaspoon ground celery seed
pinch of cayenne
5 green chillies, sliced
finely grated zest and juice of ½ lime
250 ml (9 fl oz/1 cup) white wine vinegar
2 tablespoons cornflour (cornstarch)
¼ teaspoon ground turmeric
1½ tablespoons caster (superfine) sugar

Heat the vegetable oil in a large saucepan over medium heat and sauté the onion with the salt until soft. Add the capsicum and sauté for a few minutes until starting to soften, then add the corn and sauté for another minute. Mix in the coriander, celery seed and cayenne, then take off the heat and stir through the green chillies, lime zest and juice.

For the salsa base, combine the vinegar with 250 ml (9 fl oz/1 cup) of water in a non-reactive saucepan. Put the cornflour and turmeric into a heatproof bowl, then stir in 2–3 tablespoons of the vinegar mixture to make a smooth paste. Add the sugar to the vinegar mixture, then place over medium heat and stir until the sugar has dissolved. When the mixture reaches simmering point, transfer it to a jug, then slowly pour into the cornflour paste, whisking as you go until you have a smooth, thick sauce. Leave to cool.

Pour the cooled salsa base over the vegetables and stir to coat evenly. The salsa can be served straightaway or kept in the fridge for up to a month.

If you want to bottle the salsa to store for use later in the year, or to give as a gift, pack it into sterilised jars (see page 250) and heat-process (see page 255) for 10 minutes. Unopened jars can be stored in a cool, dark place for up to 12 months; once opened, refrigerate and use within a couple of months.

AUTUMN PICNIC

We're always looking for new ways to learn about food and its sources. So one autumn the extended Cornersmith family went on an excursion to the Southern Highlands of New South Wales to forage for pine mushrooms. Led by our knowledgeable friend Diego Bonetto, affectionately known as 'The Weedy One', we were lucky to benefit from his expertise in foraging traditions.

We spent the day in the forest, identifying and picking pine mushrooms, filling crates and planning what we would do with our bounty.

At lunchtime, we celebrated our luck with a fireside picnic: Sabine cooked pine mushroom schnitzels (see page 175), which we ate with pickles, Kristen's labneh (see page 37) and bread, all washed down with plenty of cider.

After our day in the forest, we preserved all the mushrooms we couldn't eat straightaway: we pickled them, dried them and preserved them in oil and salt. Mushrooming is a great celebration of autumn, and has now become an annual Cornersmith tradition. If you're considering going mushrooming, make sure you seek advice from an expert first and never consume anything that you cannot properly identify.

You don't need to go foraging to enjoy preserving mushrooms at home, though. We also get different varieties of mushrooms from our fruit and veg supplier, so look for a mushroom grower at a farmers' market and pick their brains.

DRIED MUSHROOMS

We always dehydrate some of our mushroom loot, so we have dried mushrooms to use for the rest of the year: shiitake, porcini and pine mushrooms work well. You can do the same if you have a dehydrator or an oven that goes down to 40°C (104°F); if your oven doesn't have a setting this low, put it on its lowest setting and prop the door ajar with the handle of a wooden spoon (if you have a gas oven keep an eye on the flame to make sure it doesn't go out).

Clean the mushrooms by brushing off any dirt with a pastry brush or damp paper towel; if the stalks are too dirty to clean, cut them off and discard them. Keep smaller mushrooms whole and cut any larger ones into thick slices. Place in the dehydrator overnight, or spread the mushrooms out on a baking tray lined with baking paper, leaving enough space for the air to circulate freely around them, and dry in a very low oven for 6–10 hours, depending on how thickly you have sliced your mushrooms. The mushrooms need to be completely dried before they are stored in airtight containers, or they will go mouldy.

To rehydrate the mushrooms for use in risottos, stews and meat sauces, cover them with hot water and leave for at least half an hour. Drain the rehydrated mushrooms, then either chop or leave whole and add to your dish. Don't discard the soaking liquid; it's full of flavour, and can also be added to the dish, or used to boost soups and stocks.

MUSHROOM SALT

We've also experimented with a mushroom seasoning salt, which is lovely sprinkled on red meats, or to inject some extra mushroomy flavour to risottos or soups. Put a small handful of dehydrated mushrooms into a spice grinder and whizz to a fine powder, then combine 1 part of mushroom powder with 2 parts of pure salt. Store in a clean, dry airtight container or jar.

PINE MUSHROOM SCHNITZELS

PREPARATION TIME
25 minutes

COOKING TIME
15 minutes

SERVES 4

Pine mushrooms have a firm, almost meaty texture, and this recipe makes the most of this. Make sure you cook them for long enough, or they can taste bitter – keep the heat down to medium when frying the schnitzels, so they get the chance to cook through. These are delicious eaten straight from the pan, or served with preserved lemon aioli (see page 97) and a salad (the kale and apple one on page 135 is a good match). If you can't find pine mushrooms, try this recipe with flat field mushrooms.

12 small–medium pine mushrooms, stalks removed
2–3 free-range eggs, depending on the size of your mushrooms
2 garlic cloves, finely chopped
60 g (2¼ oz/1 cup) fresh breadcrumbs
40 g (1½ oz) almond meal
finely grated zest of 1 lemon
1 tablespoon chopped thyme
plain (all-purpose) flour, for dusting
about 80 ml (2½ fl oz/⅓ cup) olive oil

Clean the mushrooms with a pastry brush, clean cloth or damp paper towel.

Beat the eggs with the garlic and a pinch of salt in a shallow bowl. In another shallow bowl, combine the breadcrumbs, almond meal, lemon zest and thyme.

Season the mushrooms with salt and pepper, then dust lightly with flour. Dip them first in the egg mixture, and then in the crumb mixture.

Heat the olive oil in a frying pan big enough to fit all the mushrooms in a single layer – you need about a 1 cm (½ in) depth of oil in the pan. If you don't have a big enough frying pan, do this in batches, dividing the olive oil evenly between the batches and keeping the cooked schnitzels warm in a 120°C (235°F/gas mark ½) oven.

Place the mushroom schnitzels in the pan and fry over medium heat for 10–15 minutes, turning them frequently until they are crisp on the outside and cooked through. Drain on paper towel, then serve.

PREPARATION TIME
20 minutes

COOKING TIME
15 minutes

STORAGE
up to 2 weeks

MAKES
1 x 500 ml
(17 fl oz/2 cup) jar

PRESERVED MUSHROOMS IN OIL

This is based on an Italian style of preserving, where the vegetables are cooked in a vinegar brine, strained and then covered in oil. Treated this way, your mushrooms will keep for a couple of weeks in the fridge. If you like, you can also add some other flavourings. A sprig of rosemary and a few peppercorns in the bottom of each jar is a good combination, or try thyme, bay and lemon zest. Serve these mushrooms as part of an antipasto platter, or stir them through sauces – they're especially good with meat that is on the gamier side, such as venison, wallaby or duck.

250 ml (9 fl oz/1 cup) white wine vinegar
2 tablespoons salt
500 g (1 lb 2 oz) pine, field, swiss brown or chestnut mushrooms, cleaned and cut into thick slices
olive oil, to cover

Sterilise your jar (see page 250) and leave to cool completely.

Combine the vinegar and salt with 500 ml (17 fl oz/2 cups) of water in a medium non-reactive saucepan. Place over low heat and bring to a simmer, stirring to dissolve the salt.

Working in batches, place the mushroom slices into the hot brine and simmer for a minute or two until tender. Remove with a slotted spoon and squeeze out the excess liquid, before packing into the jar and covering with olive oil. Seal and keep in the fridge for up to 2 weeks.

PICKLED MUSHROOMS

Autumn is the time to pickle mushrooms. We usually use pine mushrooms or slippery jacks, but you could also try swiss brown, chestnut or king brown (also known as king oyster) mushrooms. Experiment by adding some garlic, thyme, bay leaves or peppercorns to the jars. Pickled pine mushrooms seem to develop a slightly gelatinous coating after sitting for a while. There's nothing wrong with this, and they still taste great – just rinse it off if it bothers you.

PREPARATION TIME
30 minutes

COOKING TIME
20 minutes, plus 15 minutes heat-processing

STORAGE
up to 12 months

MAKES
2 x 500 ml (17 fl oz/2 cup) jars

500 ml (17 fl oz/2 cups) white wine vinegar
55 g (2 oz/¼ cup) caster (superfine) sugar
1 teaspoon sea salt
1 kg (2 lb 4 oz) pine mushrooms or slippery jacks, cleaned

Sterilise your jars (see page 250) and leave to cool completely.

Put the vinegar, sugar, salt and 250 ml (9 fl oz/1 cup) of water in a non-reactive saucepan over low heat and stir until the sugar and salt have dissolved, then increase the heat and bring to a simmer.

Pop the whole mushrooms in the brine for a minute or two, just to soften slightly – remember the heat-processing will cook them further. Remove with a slotted spoon and pack into the jars (see page 252 for packing tips). If the mushrooms are big, slice or quarter them; otherwise, leave them whole.

Carefully fill the jars with the hot brine until the mushrooms are completely covered. Remove any air bubbles by gently tapping each jar on the work surface and sliding a butter knife or chopstick around the inside to release any hidden air pockets. You may need to add more brine or mushrooms after doing this (the liquid should reach about 1 cm/½ in from the top of the jar). Wipe the rims of the jars with a clean cloth or paper towel and seal.

Heat-process (see page 255) for 15 minutes, then store in a cool, dark place for up to 12 months. Once opened, refrigerate and use within a month.

PREPARATION TIME
20 minutes

COOKING TIME
40 minutes

SERVES 6

MAEVE'S BAKED APPLES

This is our daughter's recipe – it was the first thing she cooked for us all by herself. We were very proud.

3 apples
3 tablespoons butter
1 teaspoon ground cinnamon
6 teaspoons raw sugar
3 tablespoons honey
juice of 1 orange
ice cream, to serve

Preheat the oven to 160°C (315°F/gas mark 2–3).

Cut the apples in half across the core and scoop out the seeds to make a hollow.

Put the apples in a baking dish, then put a chunk of butter in each hollow. Sprinkle a pinch of cinnamon and a teaspoon of raw sugar over each apple. Drizzle with the honey and orange juice.

Bake the apples for 40 minutes, then give everybody half an apple and heaps of ice cream.

PREPARATION TIME
10 minutes

COOKING TIME
10 minutes

MAKES
700 ml (24 fl oz)

VANILLA CUSTARD

This version is lighter and slightly less sweet than traditional custard. With no cornflour to thicken it, it might need a bit more of your attention, but the cleaner taste that comes from using only the natural binding qualities of the egg is definitely worth the extra effort. Serve it with Franca's sugar plum buns (see opposite) or Maeve's baked apples (see page 180).

300 ml (10½ fl oz) milk
300 ml (10½ fl oz) pouring cream
1 vanilla bean, split and seeds scraped
80 g (2¾ oz) caster (superfine) sugar
4 free-range egg yolks

Put the milk, cream and vanilla bean and seeds in a small saucepan and bring to the boil over medium heat.

Meanwhile, mix the sugar and egg yolks in a medium heatproof bowl until pale and thick. Gradually pour the hot milk mixture onto the egg yolk mixture, whisking constantly.

If you're a confident custard-maker, you can now just pour the mixture back into the saucepan and stir it continuously with a spatula over medium heat until the custard thickens. Make sure it doesn't get too hot; if it goes beyond 82°C (179°F), it will curdle and taste 'eggy'. A more cautious method is to sit the bowl of custard over a saucepan of barely simmering water (ensuring the base of the bowl isn't touching the water) and cook it, stirring continuously, until it thickens enough to coat the back of a wooden spoon.

Strain the custard into a bowl or jug and serve straightaway, or you can leave the custard to cool and refrigerate it for up to 3 days, then gently reheat if you want to serve it hot.

FRANCA'S SUGAR PLUM BUNS

Franca trained as a pastry chef, and always makes us the most amazing treats – the picklery smells best on the days she works there! This is her recipe for traditional sweet buns from southern Germany, where they are eaten as a lunchtime treat, but they're also perfect for afternoon tea. This is hearty, home-style baking; comfort food for when the weather starts to get colder.

PREPARATION TIME
30 minutes, plus 1½ hours rising

COOKING TIME
20 minutes

MAKES
12 buns

350 g (12 oz/2⅓ cups) plain (all-purpose) flour
150 g (5½ oz/1 cup) wholemeal (whole-wheat) flour
2 teaspoons dried yeast
50 g (1¾ oz) caster (superfine) sugar
100 g (3½ oz) softened butter, plus 2 tablespoons melted butter
2 free-range eggs, lightly beaten
300 ml (10½ fl oz) lukewarm milk
12 large or 24 smaller sugar plums, stones removed
1 tablespoon sugar mixed with
    1 teaspoon ground cinnamon
vanilla custard (see opposite), to serve

Put the flours, yeast, sugar and a pinch of salt into the bowl of a stand mixer fitted with the dough hook and mix briefly to combine. Add the softened butter, eggs and 250 ml (9 fl oz/1 cup) of the milk and mix on low speed for 1 minute. Increase the speed to medium and knead the dough for about 10 minutes or until smooth and glossy. If making the dough by hand, combine the flours, yeast, sugar and a pinch of salt in a large bowl, then add the softened butter, eggs and 250 ml (9 fl oz/1 cup) of the milk. Mix to form a dough, then turn out onto a floured work surface and knead for at least 10 minutes or until smooth.

Shape the dough into a ball and put into a lightly oiled bowl, then cover with a clean tea towel or plastic bag and set aside in a warm place to prove for about an hour or until doubled in size.

Transfer the dough to a lightly floured work surface and punch once to knock it back, then knead briefly, just to get rid of any big air bubbles. Divide the dough into 12 even portions, then roll each one into a ball and leave to rise for another 10 minutes. Flatten each ball with the palm of your hand and put 1 large or 2 smaller sugar plums in the middle. Fold the dough over to enclose the fruit, pinching the edges together, then turn the bun over so the seam is underneath.

Preheat the oven to 200°C (400°F/gas mark 6) and brush a deep baking dish with melted butter. Place the buns in the baking dish and leave to rise again until they spring back when pressed gently, about 15–20 minutes. Mix the remaining melted butter with the rest of the milk, then brush this over the tops of the buns and sprinkle over the cinnamon sugar. Bake for 20 minutes or until well risen and golden brown, then serve warm with vanilla custard.

PERSIMMONS WITH WATTLESEED MASCARPONE

PREPARATION TIME
5 minutes

COOKING TIME
5 minutes

SERVES 4

Persimmons are eaten in two quite different ways: firmer fruit are shaved and eaten raw, while fruit with soft flesh is scooped out. Try them with bresaola (in the same way as you would serve melon with prosciutto), in salads or with roasted meats. For this simple recipe, which celebrates the flavour of the fruit, you want the softer, ripe persimmons. You could also serve the grilled persimmons with ricotta cream instead (see below).

1 tablespoon honey
juice of ½ lime
4 ripe persimmons, tops cut off
pinch of ground wattleseed or freshly grated nutmeg
100 g (3½ oz) mascarpone

Preheat the grill (broiler) to high. Drizzle the honey and lime juice over the cut fruit, then place on a baking tray under the grill and cook until golden brown.

Fold the wattleseed or nutmeg through the mascarpone and serve with the warm persimmons.

KRISTEN'S RICOTTA CREAM

PREPARATION TIME
20 minutes

SERVES 6

You can serve this with any seasonal fruit, but Kristen's favourite combination is figs and honey.

300 g (10½ oz) ricotta
1 teaspoon caster (superfine) sugar
dash of milk, if needed

Put the ricotta and sugar into a mixing bowl.

Using a stick blender, blitz until the ricotta becomes smooth and glossy. Depending on the power of the blender, this will take 10–20 minutes.

If you are having trouble working the ricotta into a cream, add a dash of milk.

Serve with seasonal fruit.

PREPARATION TIME
25 minutes

COOKING TIME
50 minutes

MAKES
1 x 20 cm
(8 in) cake

STEPH'S GINGERBREAD LAYER CAKE WITH RHUBARB, RICOTTA & WALNUTS

This is another one of Steph's pretty seasonal cakes.

400 g (14 oz/2 ⅔ cups) plain (all-purpose) flour, sifted
2 teaspoons bicarbonate of soda (baking soda), sifted
1 teaspoon baking powder, sifted
2½ teaspoons ground ginger
250 g (9 oz) brown sugar
200 g (7 oz) unsalted butter
350 g (12 oz/1 cup) treacle or molasses
2 free-range eggs, lightly beaten
1 quantity rhubarb and hibuscus (see page 58) and its syrup
6 walnuts, ideally new-season ones, shaved very thinly on a mandoline
edible flowers, to decorate – optional

RICOTTA FILLING
700 g (1 lb 9 oz) ricotta
375 ml (13 fl oz/1½ cups) pouring cream, whipped to soft peaks
1 vanilla bean, split and seeds scraped
finely grated zest of 1 lemon
3 tablespoons caster (superfine) sugar

Preheat the oven to 180°C (350°F/gas mark 4). Grease and line two 20 cm (8 in) round cake tins.

Sift the flour, bicarbonate of soda, baking powder and ginger into a large bowl, then stir in the brown sugar. In a small saucepan, melt the butter and add the treacle. Leave to cool slightly, then mix in the eggs. Pour into the flour mixture and mix until combined. Lastly, fold through 250 ml (9 fl oz/1 cup) of hot (but not boiling) water from the kettle.

Divide the batter evenly between the two tins and bake for 40–50 minutes or until a skewer inserted in the centre comes out clean. Leave to cool completely.

For the ricotta filling, fold all the ingredients together in a bowl until smooth, then chill the mixture until you're ready to assemble the cake.

Put the syrup from the poached rhubarb into a small saucepan and simmer until reduced to a thick but still pourable syrup.

To assemble, cut the dome off both cakes, then cut each cake horizontally into two even layers, giving you four layers in total (you only need three layers here, so save the other for a trifle). Using a palette knife, spread the first layer of cake with some ricotta filling, then place a third of the rhubarb on top, followed by another layer of cake. Repeat with the remaining layers, finishing with a thick layer of ricotta and the last third of the rhubarb. Scatter with walnut shavings, then drizzle with the rhubarb syrup and top with edible flowers, if using.

WINTER

PREPARATION TIME
25 minutes

COOKING TIME
50 minutes

MAKES
1 loaf

PURPLE CARROT LOAF

One of our pet hates is bad banana bread – the super-sweet, oily kind you often find in airport cafes. When we opened Cornersmith, we were determined to have a sweet loaf on the menu that was a good and relatively healthy breakfast option.

We baked a lot of loaves before finally finding inspiration in one of our favourite books, the Rose Bakery's *Breakfast, Lunch, Tea*. Our version uses purple carrots, coarsely grated for added texture, but the recipe works just as well with beetroot, sweet potato or pumpkin. Just experiment with what you have around.

Our kids love a slice of this in their school lunch boxes – we just leave out the nuts and replace them with dark chocolate buttons or raisins. At the cafe, we serve it as a breakfast loaf, either fresh from the tin with lots of butter or toasted with a dollop of ricotta, honey and a scattering of toasted nuts.

300 g (10½ oz/2 cups) plain (all-purpose) flour
1 heaped teaspoon baking powder
½ teaspoon bicarbonate of soda (baking soda)
½ teaspoon salt
1 teaspoon ground cinnamon
4 free-range eggs
225 g (8 oz) caster (superfine) sugar
300 ml (10½ fl oz) sunflower oil
5 purple carrots, coarsely grated
150 g (5½ oz) walnuts or hazelnuts, finely chopped, plus extra sliced nuts

Preheat the oven to 180°C (350°F/gas mark 4). Line the base of a 26 cm (10½ in) loaf (bar) tin with baking paper. Sift the flour, baking powder, bicarbonate of soda, salt and cinnamon into a large bowl.

Using electric beaters, beat the eggs and sugar until pale, thick and frothy. Slowly add the sunflower oil and continue beating for a few more minutes until smooth and well combined.

Using a spatula or large metal spoon, mix in the carrots, then fold in the flour mixture and the nuts. Pour the batter into the prepared tin, scatter over the sliced nuts and bake for 45–50 minutes or until a skewer inserted in the centre of the loaf comes out clean. Leave to cool before serving.

TRADING

Our trading days began before Cornersmith, when Alex was at home with two young kids...

'My friend Jaimee and I were teaching ourselves to preserve. When the kids got cabin fever we'd wander the streets, and I started noticing all the heavily laden fruit trees and bountiful vegetable patches in the surrounding streets. As the kids got older and my walks got longer, I realised that Marrickville, Dulwich Hill and all along the Cooks River were full of produce. In winter, piles of oranges and lemons would accumulate in backyards and spill out onto the footpath. In summer, the footpaths were stained with decaying mulberries and half-eaten figs.

As my preserving bug took hold, I started knocking on doors and asking whoever answered if they used their fruit – and if not, could I come and pick it? I always took the kids, so I didn't seem completely nuts! We gathered a few buckets of cumquats from a guy down the road; bags of bitter oranges from another neighbour; and lemons, rosemary and a bag of chokos from an elderly Greek lady, who was very keen to pass on her tips. Jaimee and I then got to work bottling the produce, learning as we went. When we were done, we'd drop off a jar to each of the growers and fill up our cupboards with the rest. Soon the word spread, and I began to find parcels of home-grown produce on my doorstep.'

Then, when we opened Cornersmith, we wondered how people would take to an informal trading system, so we put up a sign in the shop saying that we were looking for home-grown backyard produce to trade. The response was incredible: people came with baskets of herbs, tubs of mulberries and mountains of citrus fruit. Steve, who lives just across the road from the cafe, brought in a bag of beautiful rocket every morning in exchange for his coffee. We were overwhelmed by people's generosity, and the names of our home-growers were written up on a board so they could grab a coffee or take home a jar of pickles in return. For us, the whole experience demonstrated that, as a community, we need places where we can meet, share ideas, swap knowledge and talk about food.

Everything went on the menu. We put the greens in our salads, pounded nasturtium leaves for pesto, made passionfruit into curd, and added mulberries to our milkshakes. We preserved lemons and limes, cooked up every kind of marmalade imaginable, and stockpiled chilli paste. The trading system came to our rescue that first year. We have a cheese and pickle sandwich on the menu, but we ran out of pickles before the season started again. As winter closed in, we were wondering what else we could pickle that would work on a sandwich. Then someone dropped in some chokos, and the answer was clear: they make the best pickles (see page 227). We put a sign up in the shop and a note on Instagram, and sure enough the chokos started rolling in.

Since then, it has just got bigger and bigger. Last year, we traded over 500 kilos (about half a ton) of citrus fruit, along with vast quantities of chokos, cumquats and beautiful quinces, boxes of rangpur limes and mountains of herbs. We've set up trading guidelines – a box of fruit or veg in exchange for a jar of pickles is generally the rule of thumb. But the majority of people just want to see their produce go to a good home; for it not to be wasted, to see it being used by the community, and to have a good story to tell.

MANDARIN & STAR ANISE JAM

One winter we received so many mandarins from our customers' backyards that we simply couldn't face making another batch of marmalade, so we made citrus jam instead. What a winner! Since then, this has become one of our favourite jams. It's also a big seller at the markets, and die-hard fans now know to buy enough jars to keep them going all year before we sell out.

PREPARATION TIME
30 minutes

COOKING TIME
1½ hours

STORAGE
up to 12 months

MAKES
4–5 x 300 ml
(10½ fl oz) jars

1.5 kg (3 lb 5 oz) mandarins
3 star anise, plus 4–5 extra for decoration
200 ml (7 fl oz) lemon juice – about 2 juicy lemons' worth
1 kg (2 lb 4 oz) caster (superfine) sugar

Peel the mandarins, then cut in half around their middle and remove the pips. Don't worry – this is the only time-consuming part of this jam-making. But if you get sick of it, a few pips are all right; they contain a lot of pectin, which will help your jam to set, and you can just pick them off your toast.

Break up the mandarins into small chunks and put them into a jam pan or wide, heavy-based saucepan. Cover with 2.5 litres (87 fl oz/10 cups) of water and add the star anise. Place over medium heat and simmer slowly until the mandarin segments are soft and breaking down and the liquid has reduced by a third, about 30–45 minutes.

Meanwhile, sterilise your jars (see page 250).

Add the lemon juice and sugar to the mandarins and stir until the sugar has completely dissolved. Turn up the heat and boil rapidly until setting point is reached (see page 250), about 40 minutes. Keep an eye on the jam while it's cooking, and stir occasionally to prevent it burning. Remove from the heat and let the jam sit for 5 minutes.

Carefully pour the hot jam into the hot jars – we like to put a star anise on top of the jam in each jar. Wipe the rims with a clean damp cloth or paper towel, then put the lids on. Store in a cool, dark place for up to 12 months. Once opened, refrigerate and use within 2 months.

JAM TRIANGLES

If you have some left-over sweet pastry (see page 243), roll it out to a 3 mm (⅛ in) thickness, then use a 7 cm (2¾ in) round cutter or a drinking glass to cut out circles. Put a heaped teaspoon of jam in the centre of each circle. Lightly brush the edges of the pastry circle with water and then fold up in three places to form a triangle, pinching together the seams at the corners. Place the jam triangles on a baking tray lined with baking paper and chill for 30 minutes. Sprinkle with cinnamon or other spices before baking at 180°C (350°F; gas mark 4) for 15 minutes or until golden, then cool on a wire rack. These will keep in an airtight container for up to 2 days, or a couple of days longer in the fridge.

PREPARATION TIME
30 minutes

COOKING TIME
1 hour

STORAGE
up to 12 months

MAKES
4 x 300 ml
(10½ fl oz) jars

CARROT JAM

Jaimee has been trying to persuade us to have carrot jam on the menu for many years. This bright orange, fresh and zingy, Iranian-influenced jam is the one that changed our minds about vegetable jams, and convinced us that they can be a delicious alternative to fruit jam. Spread over generously buttered toast, or serve with fresh curd, labneh, ricotta or goat's cheese.

1 kg (2 lb 4 oz) carrots, peeled
3 cardamom pods, smashed and seeds extracted
juice and finely grated zest of 5–6 limes
1 kg (2 lb 4 oz) caster (superfine) sugar
1 teaspoon salt

Grate the carrots on the coarse side of a box grater.

Put the carrots into a jam pan or a large wide saucepan with the cardamom seeds. Pour in 3 litres (105 fl oz/12 cups) of water and bring to the boil, then reduce the heat and simmer for 30 minutes or until the carrots are very soft.

Add the lime juice and zest, sugar and salt. Stir until the sugar has completely dissolved, then turn up the heat and boil rapidly until setting point (see page 250) is reached, about 30 minutes. Leave to cool slightly.

Meanwhile, sterilise your jars (see page 250).

Carefully pour the hot jam into the hot sterilised jars. Wipe the rims of the jars clean with paper towel, then seal.

This jam can be eaten immediately, or stored in a cool, dark place for up to 12 months. Once a jar has been opened, refrigerate and use within 3 months.

BRUSSELS SLAW WITH WHEY DRESSING, POMELO, HAZELNUTS & POACHED EGG

PREPARATION TIME
20 minutes

SERVES 4

We serve lots of this in the cafe as a healthy breakfast or light lunch, often with a little pecorino or parmesan shaved on top. If you like, you could mix in some shredded cabbage and leave out the egg for a simple salad to serve alongside meat dishes or in a sandwich. Buttermilk, kefir or yoghurt can be used in place of whey in the dressing.

80 ml (2½ fl oz/⅓ cup) whey
1 tablespoon apple balsamic vinegar or cider vinegar
125 ml (4 fl oz/½ cup) olive oil
400 g (14 oz) brussels sprouts, thinly shaved
1 pomelo, segmented and cut or torn into pieces
55 g (2 oz) toasted hazelnuts, coarsely chopped, plus extra to serve
2 handfuls (1 cup) mint leaves, torn
4 poached free-range eggs (see page 261)

To make the dressing, combine the whey, vinegar and olive oil in a screw-top jar. Season with salt and pepper, then put the lid on and shake well to mix.

In a large bowl, combine the brussels sprouts, pomelo, hazelnuts and mint. Pour over the dressing and toss gently, then check the seasoning.

Serve the salad in shallow bowls, with a poached egg on top and garnished with the extra hazelnuts.

PREPARATION TIME
40 minutes

COOKING TIME
55 minutes

SERVES 4–6
or up to 8 as finger food

CHARD & WILD GREENS PIE

This is our version of a traditional Greek recipe, inspired by a friend of Sabine's who, on a visit to Crete, saw women preparing these pies everywhere she went. Greece has a long tradition of foraging for bitter greens, which are highly nutritious and considered good for the digestion. Winter is the time to go foraging for bitter greens in the city – here in Marrickville, we can find dandelions and warrigal greens. Just make sure you know what you're picking, and wash everything well. If you're not up for foraging, look for chard varieties, herbs and bitter greens at farmers' markets.

The pie can be served warm or cold with a squeeze of lemon juice or a dollop of yoghurt.

To guarantee golden and crispy filo, the greens for the filling must be very, very dry – the best way is to wring out the cooked greens using your hands. If you like, you can make the filling or even the whole pie a day in advance.

1 bunch rainbow chard or swiss chard, leaves removed from stems
50 ml (1¾ fl oz) olive oil
8 shallots, thinly sliced into rings
1 quarter preserved lemon (see page 214), rind only, finely chopped
80 g (2¾ oz/1 bunch) mint, leaves picked and finely chopped
150 g (5½ oz/1 bunch) parsley, leaves picked and finely chopped
2 handfuls foraged or bought bitter greens, finely chopped
good pinch of freshly grated nutmeg
200 g (7 oz) sheep's or goat's fetta, finely crumbled
4 free-range eggs, lightly beaten
1½ tablespoons melted butter
6 sheets filo pastry
lemon halves, to serve

Bring a large saucepan of salted water to the boil. Add the chard leaves and blanch for 5 minutes or until they soften. Drain and refresh under cold running water, then drain again. Use your hands to squeeze the chard as dry as possible, then chop finely.

Thinly slice the chard stems. Heat a tablespoon of the olive oil in a frying pan over medium heat, add the chard stems and fry for about 3–5 minutes or until they soften. Add the shallots and cook for 2 minutes, then add the preserved lemon and season with a little salt (not too much, as the preserved lemon and fetta will be quite salty) and pepper.

In a large bowl, combine the herbs, chopped chard leaves and bitter greens, along with half of the chard stem mixture. Season with nutmeg and pepper, then add three-quarters of the fetta and all of the beaten egg. Thoroughly mix everything together.

Preheat the oven to 180°C (350°F/gas mark 4). Combine the melted butter with the remaining olive oil in a small bowl. Brush the base and sides of a 22 cm (8½ in) non-stick ovenproof frying pan with the butter and oil.

You need to work quickly with filo, or it dries out and becomes brittle. Lay a sheet of filo on a clean, dry surface, brush with the melted butter and oil, then place in the pan, brushed-side up and slightly off-centre, so it partially covers the base and overhangs one side of the pan. Continue in the same way with the second, third and fourth sheets, creating an overlapping cross shape with pastry hanging over the edge of the pan all the way round. Place the fifth sheet of filo in the same position as the first, just to stabilise the pie.

Spoon the filling into the pie case, spreading it out evenly. Sprinkle over the rest of the chard stem mixture and the remaining fetta. Now, one by one, fold the overhanging ends of the pastry sheets over the filling, brushing the top of each one with butter and oil as you go. Lay the sixth sheet of filo on top, tucking in the edges, then brush with butter and oil.

Bake the pie for 40 minutes, turning it around a few times so it browns evenly. Remove from the oven and let it sit in the pan for about 5 minutes, then turn it out, upside down, onto a board. Cut into slices or squares and serve with lemon halves for squeezing.

CARROT & ORANGE SOUP

PREPARATION TIME
20 minutes

COOKING TIME
1 hour

SERVES 4

Winter is soup season, and in this one the orange really enhances the sweetness of the carrot to make a soup that's hearty without being too heavy. Plus it's a nice change from pumpkin soup. It's important to season this soup well at the beginning, as you'll be adding a lot of liquid later on.

Try making this soup with parsnips instead – it won't have the same rich saffron colour, but it will have a nutty, more earthy flavour.

2½ tablespoons olive oil, plus extra for drizzling
30 g (1 oz) butter
2 large brown onions, thinly sliced
2–3 garlic cloves, thinly sliced
1 cm (½ in) knob of ginger, thinly sliced
3–4 thyme sprigs
2 bay leaves
zest of 3 oranges, peeled in long strips with a vegetable peeler
1 kg (2 lb 4 oz) carrots, thinly sliced
juice of 3 oranges
1.5 litres (52 fl oz/6 cups) vegetable or chicken stock or water
½ teaspoon chopped thyme leaves
2 teaspoons chopped pistachio nuts
sheep's yoghurt, to serve – optional

Heat the olive oil and butter in a large saucepan over medium heat. Add the onions and a couple of pinches of salt and pepper then sauté until soft. Add the garlic, ginger, thyme sprigs, bay leaves and orange zest and sauté for another 5 minutes.

Add the carrot and a bit more salt and cook for another 3–5 minutes or until the carrot is starting to soften. Add the orange juice and reduce until almost no liquid is left, then add the stock or water. Cover with a lid and bring to the boil, then reduce the heat and simmer for 35–40 minutes or until the carrot is completely soft.

Remove from the heat and let the soup sit for 5 minutes before removing the thyme sprigs and bay leaves. Transfer the soup to a blender or food processor and blend until smooth.

Serve the soup in bowls, drizzled with olive oil and sprinkled with the thyme and pistachios. You may also like to add a dollop of sheep's yoghurt, which goes very well with this soup.

PREPARATION TIME
10 minutes

COOKING TIME
10 minutes

SERVES 1

CORNERSMITH REUBEN-STYLE SANDWICH

We always have this sandwich, our tribute to the famous American deli classic, on the menu in winter. With mustard, sauerkraut and pickles, this is a celebration of the craft of preserving, and of curing meat in the time-honoured way – we use the beautiful corned beef made with minimal sulphites from our friends around the corner at Feather and Bone.

2 slices rye bread – with caraway is nice
1 teaspoon aioli (see page 97), made without the preserved lemon
½ teaspoon Cornersmith mustard (see page 159) or other grainy mustard
2–3 tablespoons Jaimee's sauerkraut (see page 149) or other sauerkraut
bread and butter cucumber pickles (see page 111) or other cucumber pickles, to taste
2–3 thin slices corned beef or pastrami
2 slices gruyere or similar cheese
snow pea shoots or lettuce

Place the slices of bread on a board. Spread aioli on one slice and mustard on the other. Evenly spread sauerkraut onto the mustard-spread slice of bread, then lay some pickles on top, followed by the corned beef or pastrami and cheese. Season with pepper, then place the aioli-spread slice of bread on top and gently press down.

Place in a sandwich press and cook until golden brown on both sides. You might have to carefully flip it a couple of times to make sure the cheese gets really melty. (If you don't have a sandwich press, pan-fry your sandwich until golden on both sides, then finish under a hot grill/broiler to melt the cheese if needed.)

Take your Reuben out of the sandwich press, ease it apart and add some pea shoots or lettuce. Put it back together, cut in half and serve straightaway.

ROASTED BEETROOT & RHUBARB SALAD WITH FETTA

PREPARATION TIME
30 minutes

COOKING TIME
1 hour

SERVES 4

This unusual combination makes a warming winter salad, with the earthiness of the beetroot offset by the tart rhubarb and salty fetta. Eat this by itself or as a side dish with lamb.

If you can find them, use several different varieties of beetroot. And if the leaves are still attached, reserve two big handfuls of any smaller leaves that aren't too leathery and add them to the salad just before serving.

- ½ **teaspoon black peppercorns**
- ½ **teaspoon coriander seeds**
- ½ **teaspoon allspice berries**
- 1.5 kg (3 lb 5 oz/2 bunches) small–medium beetroot (beets)
- zest of ½ orange, in small strips
- 2 thyme or lemon thyme sprigs
- 2 oregano sprigs
- 1 garlic clove, thinly sliced
- 2 handfuls coarse salt
- 300 g (10½ oz) rhubarb – about 3–4 stalks
- 35 g (1¼ oz) brown sugar
- juice of 1 lemon
- 1 tablespoon sherry vinegar
- 2½ tablespoons olive oil
- small handful (¼ cup, firmly packed) dill fronds
- small handful (¼ cup, firmly packed) mint leaves
- 70 g (2½ oz) fetta, crumbled

Preheat the oven to 200°C (400°F/gas mark 6).

Coarsely crush the peppercorns, coriander seeds and allspice using a pestle and mortar. Cut out 20 cm (8 in) squares of baking paper and foil, then place one medium or two smaller beetroot on each square. Evenly divide the crushed spices, orange zest, thyme, oregano and garlic between the squares, season with fine salt and wrap up to form parcels.

Spread the coarse salt on a baking tray (this stops the beetroot burning on the bottom), then place the parcels on the salt and roast for 45–60 minutes or until the beetroot are cooked through – you should be able to easily insert the tip of a knife into the centre.

Meanwhile, trim the rhubarb and cut into 5 cm (2 in) lengths. Place in a bowl with the brown sugar and lemon juice and toss. Spread the rhubarb out in a single layer on a baking tray lined with baking paper and roast for 10–12 minutes until soft-ish but not totally falling apart.

For the vinaigrette, put the sherry vinegar and olive oil in a screw-top jar. Season with salt and pepper, then put the lid on and shake until combined.

When the beetroot are cool enough to handle, peel and cut into wedges. Tear the dill and mint into smaller pieces. Place the beetroot, rhubarb and half of the dill and mint in a bowl, then pour over the vinaigrette and toss gently.

Serve the salad on a platter, topped with the crumbled fetta, the remaining dill and mint and any reserved small, tender leaves from the beetroot.

PREPARATION TIME
20 minutes

STORAGE
several years

MAKES
2 x 500 ml
(17 fl oz/2 cup) jars

PRESERVED LEMONS OR LIMES

Every home cook should know how to make preserved lemons or limes – they're the most straightforward and cheapest of all the preserves. All you need is lemons or limes and salt!

Once you have a jar of these on the go, you'll wonder how you lived without them: use to pep up a white bean mash (see page 223), chard and wild greens pie (see page 204) or lamb tagine (see page 228), stir through aioli (see page 97), or smash into avocado and serve on toast.

1 kg (2 lb 4 oz) lemons or limes – if using limes, you
    may need a few extra if they aren't particularly juicy
100–150 g (3½ –5½ oz) salt

FOR EACH JAR OF PRESERVED LEMONS (OPTIONAL):
1 bay leaf or 1 cinnamon stick and 2 cloves
1 allspice berry
5 black peppercorns

FOR EACH JAR OF PRESERVED LIMES (OPTIONAL):
1 red chilli
½ teaspoon coriander seeds
5 black peppercorns

First sterilise your jars (see page 250), then leave to cool completely.

Cut the lemons or limes into quarters, or halves if very small. Place a tablespoon of salt into the bottom of each jar. Put a few layers of lemon or lime quarters into the jar, pressing down as you go to release the fruit's juices.

Slide your chosen spices down the side of each jar. Sprinkle over another layer of salt, then add another layer of lemon or lime quarters and repeat these layers until the jar is full. Remember to keep pushing down as you go. The fruit needs to be completely covered in salty juice – if your fruit hasn't released enough of its own juices, squeeze a few extra and pour in this juice to cover.

Leave 1 cm (½ in) of space between the top of the fruit and the lid of the jar – you don't want the salty fruit touching the lid or it will corrode the metal. Seal the jars and let them sit in a cool, dark place for 6 weeks.

You know your lemons or limes are preserved when the salt has completely dissolved into a gel-like liquid. Preserved lemons and limes will keep for years, but opened jars are best stored in the fridge (if the top layer of fruit looks discoloured, just discard it and the rest should be fine to use).

ROASTED SPICED CAULIFLOWER SALAD

This salad or side dish, with its layers of flavour and texture, is a happy result of our 'minimal waste' policy. Rather than throwing away the cauliflower stems, we pickle them and then toss them with the roasted florets: roasting brings out the sweetness of the cauliflower, which contrasts with the acidity of the pickled stems. Pickled grapes, almonds and herbs bring this salad together beautifully. If you don't have any pickled grapes, you could use fresh grapes or currants. Cooked grains such as quinoa, freekeh, farro, etc, make a delicious addition.

PREPARATION TIME
20 minutes, plus at least 30 minutes pickling

COOKING TIME
30 minutes

SERVES 4

- 1 cauliflower, head broken into small florets, stem thinly sliced on a mandoline
- 1 teaspoon coriander seeds
- 1 teaspoon cumin seeds
- ½ teaspoon yellow mustard seeds
- ½ teaspoon fennel seeds
- 1½ teaspoons smoked paprika
- pinch of cayenne
- pinch of ground turmeric
- ½ teaspoon salt
- 100 ml (3½ fl oz) olive oil
- ½ small red onion, thinly sliced
- 2 tablespoons chopped pickled red grapes (see page 164)
- 2 tablespoons chopped toasted almonds
- 1 large handful (¾ cup, firmly packed) mixed herb leaves, such as mint, dill and parsley
- juice of 1–2 lemons

QUICK-PICKLING LIQUID
- 2 teaspoons salt
- 75 g (2½ oz/⅓ cup) caster (superfine) sugar
- 125 ml (4 fl oz/½ cup) white wine vinegar or cider vinegar
- 250 ml (9 fl oz/1 cup) boiling water, cooled down for 5 minutes

Preheat the oven to 200°C (400°F/gas mark 6) and line a large baking tray with baking paper.

To make the quick-pickling liquid, stir the salt and sugar into the vinegar in a large non-reactive bowl until dissolved. Pour in the cooled boiled water, then add the sliced cauliflower stem and mix well. Leave to pickle for at least 30 minutes, then drain just before adding to the salad.

Toast the coriander, cumin, mustard and fennel seeds in a dry frying pan over medium heat until fragrant. Let them cool down, then grind to a powder using a spice grinder or pestle and mortar. Transfer to a large bowl and stir through the paprika, cayenne, turmeric, salt and olive oil.

Add the cauliflower florets to the bowl and combine really well with the spice and oil mixture. Spread out the florets on the prepared baking tray and bake for 20–25 minutes or until golden and crispy.

In a large bowl, combine the roasted cauliflower florets, pickled cauliflower stem, onion, grapes, almonds and herbs. Season with salt and pepper and add lemon juice to taste.

PREPARATION TIME
45 minutes

COOKING TIME
10 minutes,
plus 15 minutes
heat-processing

STORAGE
up to 12 months

MAKES
2 × 500 ml
(17 fl oz/2 cup) jars

PICKLED FENNEL WITH CHILLI

Cornersmith's all-time favourite winter pickle! We use this on sandwiches with salami, chilli and ricotta, tossed through salads – especially potato salad (see page 146) – or with barbecued fish.

Once you've finished eating the pickles, keep the jar of brine in the fridge. Whisked with some extra virgin olive oil, it makes a great salad dressing.

2 large fennel bulbs
1 brown onion, sliced
1 teaspoon yellow mustard seeds
1 teaspoon chilli flakes or chopped fresh red chilli
1 teaspoon fennel seeds

BRINE
500 ml (17 fl oz/2 cups) white wine vinegar
110 g (3¾ oz/½ cup) caster (superfine) sugar
½ teaspoon salt

First, sterilise your jars (see page 250).

Cut the fennel into long thin strips – you can use all of it, including the core, stems and fronds. Mix the fennel and onion together in a bowl. Sprinkle over the spices and mix through with your hands.

Make a brine by putting the vinegar, sugar, salt and 250 ml (9 fl oz/1 cup) of water into a non-reactive saucepan over low heat. Stir to dissolve the sugar, then increase the heat and bring to the boil. Let it bubble for 2–3 minutes, then remove from the heat.

When the jars are cool enough to handle, use small tongs or clean hands to carefully pack the fennel mixture into the jars. The jars should be full but not over-packed – the brine needs to cover every strip of fennel, and if they are packed too tightly the brine won't be able to get into every nook and cranny (see page 252 for more on packing techniques).

Carefully fill the jars with the hot brine until the fennel is completely covered. Remove any air bubbles by gently tapping each jar on the work surface and sliding a butter knife or chopstick around the inside to release any hidden air pockets. You may need to add more brine or fennel after doing this (the liquid should reach about 1 cm/½ in from the top of the jar). Wipe the rims of the jars with paper towel and seal.

Heat-process (see page 255) for 15 minutes, then store in a cool, dark place for up to 12 months. Let the jars of pickled fennel mature for a few weeks before opening them, then keep in the fridge and use within 3 months.

WHITE BEAN & PRESERVED LEMON MASH

PREPARATION TIME
15 minutes, plus overnight soaking

COOKING TIME
1–1½ hours

SERVES
4 as a dip for sharing

This tangy and lemony, hummus-like dip can be served simply with herbs and sprouts. At Cornersmith we pile it on toast for a savoury breakfast, but you could also make it more substantial by topping it with spiced pork and veal with pomegranate syrup (see page 86) to create a variation on the classic Lebanese dish of hummus with minced lamb.

100 ml (3½ fl oz) olive oil, plus extra for drizzling
1 large brown onion, thinly sliced
3 garlic cloves, thinly sliced
1 thyme sprig
1 marjoram sprig
1 bay leaf
3 teaspoons finely chopped preserved lemon rind
200 g (7 oz) dried white beans, soaked overnight
juice of 1–2 lemons
mixed sprouts and herbs, to serve

Heat 2 tablespoons of the oil in a large saucepan over medium heat. Add the onion, garlic, thyme, marjoram, bay leaf and 2 teaspoons of the preserved lemon rind and cook, stirring, until soft and fragrant. Add the drained beans and cover with water, then bring to the boil. Reduce the heat to a simmer and cook, with the lid on, for 1–1½ hours or until the beans are very tender. Drain the beans, reserving the cooking liquid but discarding the herbs and bay leaf.

Put the beans in a blender or food processor with 60 ml (2 fl oz/¼ cup) of their cooking liquid and the juice of 1 lemon. Season with salt and pepper and blend until smooth then, with the motor running, slowly add the remaining oil in a steady stream.

Check the seasoning, adding more lemon juice or preserved lemon rind, if desired – it should be quite lemony-tasting.

To serve, drizzle with olive oil and garnish with sprouts and herbs.

PREPARATION TIME
30 minutes

COOKING TIME
5 minutes

STORAGE
up to 6 months

MAKES
4 x 300 ml
(10½ fl oz) jars

FERMENTED CARROTS

Follow these same steps to ferment any sturdy vegetables you have on hand: try beetroot (beets), radishes, kohlrabi or cauliflower florets.

These are great tossed through a salad. They're also surprisingly sweet. If you're ever going to get a kid to eat fermented vegetables, this would be the place to start.

10 g (¼ oz) salt
500 g (1 lb 2 oz) carrots, thinly sliced
1 brown onion, thinly sliced
40 g (1½ oz) fresh turmeric, finely grated
40 g (1½ oz) ginger, finely grated

Make a brine by adding the salt to 500 ml (17 fl oz/2 cups) water in a non-reactive saucepan. Bring to the boil, then remove from the heat and leave to cool to room temperature.

Meanwhile, sterilise your jars (see page 250) and leave them to cool completely. Mix together your carrots, onions, turmeric and ginger.

Pack the carrot mixture into the jars (see page 252 for more on packing techniques), then fill the jars with the brine until the vegetables are completely covered. Wipe the rims of the jars with paper towel and seal.

Let the jars sit at room temperature, but out of direct sunlight, for 2–4 days. During this time, the lids will start to pop up, which is a sign of the fermenting process (see pages 256–259 for some fermenting tips). Transfer the jars to the fridge and leave for a week before using. Refrigerated, the fermented carrots will keep for up to 6 months.

CHOKO PICKLES

We've tried dozens of different ways to use up all the chokos that get dropped off: choko chutney, choko kimchi, choko jam. But we've reached the conclusion that the best thing to do with chokos is to make pickles. Chokos don't have much flavour of their own, so they readily absorb whatever you put in with them – the turmeric really lifts the colour, and the pickles can end up a bit grey and unappealing-looking without it.

Chokos also have a great texture for pickling: they maintain their shape and crunch in the jar, plus these guys are still good after a year in the pantry. They're great with labneh (see page 37) and crackers, on a ham sandwich, or with oily fish.

PREPARATION TIME
45 minutes, plus at least 1–2 hours salting

COOKING TIME
10 minutes, plus 15 minutes heat-processing

STORAGE
up to 12 months

MAKES
2 x 500 ml (17 fl oz/2 cup) jars

800 g (1 lb 12 oz) chokos (chayote)
1 tablespoon salt
2 lemon slices
2 garlic cloves
2 bay leaves
a few black peppercorns

BRINE
500 ml (17 fl oz/2 cups) white wine vinegar
110 g (3¾ oz/½ cup) caster (superfine) sugar
¼ teaspoon ground turmeric

If your chokos are young, they shouldn't need to be peeled, but if they've been sitting on the vine for too long their skin gets tough, so it's better to peel the older ones. Cut the chokos into long thin strips, discarding the seeds and core, then put into a bowl. Sprinkle over the salt, mix well with your hands and leave to sit for an hour or two (or overnight). This will draw out any excess moisture and help to keep the chokos crunchy. Transfer to a large colander and leave to drain thoroughly.

Meanwhile, sterilise your jars (see page 250).

Make a brine by putting the vinegar, sugar, turmeric and 250 ml (9 fl oz/1 cup) of water into a non-reactive saucepan over low heat. Stir to dissolve the sugar, then increase the heat and bring to the boil. Let it bubble for 2–3 minutes.

When the jars are cool enough to handle, use small tongs or clean hands to carefully pack the drained chokos into the jars, adding a lemon slice, garlic clove, bay leaf and a couple of peppercorns to each jar. The jars should be full but not over-packed – the brine needs to cover every strip of choko, and if they are packed too tightly the brine won't be able to get into every nook and cranny (see page 252 for more on packing techniques).

Carefully fill the jars with the hot brine until the chokos are completely covered. Remove any air bubbles by gently tapping each jar on the work surface and sliding a butter knife or chopstick around the inside to release any hidden air pockets. You may need to add more brine or chokos after doing this (the liquid should reach about 1 cm/½ in from the top of the jar). Wipe the rims of the jars with paper towel and seal.

Heat-process (see page 255) for 15 minutes, then store in a cool, dark place for up to 12 months. Once opened, refrigerate and use within a few months.

PREPARATION TIME
30 minutes, plus at least 2 hours (or overnight) soaking and marinating

COOKING TIME
2–2½ hours

SERVES 4

LAMB TAGINE WITH PRUNES & FRESH TURMERIC

Laden with spice and dried fruit, this tagine makes a hearty winter meal. If you fancy a change from couscous, try it with freekeh, a smoky green wheat from the Middle East that's now grown in Australia as well. A spoonful of yoghurt is a nice addition too.

With the end of winter in sight, we start thinking up ways of using up our bottled tomatoes, to free up some cupboard space for next summer's batch. And, as the new season's prunes have just come in from 'our' prune farmer, Roy Duffell of Prickle Hill Produce in south-western New South Wales, this fits the bill. We like to use fresh turmeric for its intense colour and extraordinary flavour, but if you can't find it, substitute half the amount of ground turmeric.

2 star anise
4 cloves
1 teaspoon coriander seeds
1 teaspoon caraway seeds
2 teaspoons smoked paprika
900 g (2 lb) lamb shoulder, cut into 5 cm (2 in) cubes
12–16 prunes, stones removed
2 tablespoons olive oil
1 large brown onion, thinly sliced
2 garlic cloves, thinly sliced
1 teaspoon grated ginger
1 teaspoon grated turmeric
1 cinnamon stick
4 small carrots, thickly sliced
1 tablespoon honey
700 g (1 lb 9 oz) bottled tomatoes (see page 105) or good-quality tinned tomatoes
3 strips of orange zest
1 bay leaf
600–700 ml (21–24 fl oz) chicken or beef stock or water
1 tablespoon coarsely chopped parsley
1 tablespoon chopped toasted almonds
1 teaspoon finely chopped preserved lemon rind
couscous or freekeh, to serve

Put the star anise, cloves and coriander and caraway seeds into a spice grinder and grind to a fine powder, then stir in the smoked paprika. Place half of this spice mix in a large bowl, add the lamb and mix well, then set aside to marinate for at least 2 hours, but preferably overnight. In another bowl, soak the prunes in water for the same amount of time.

Just before cooking, season the marinated lamb with salt and drain the prunes, reserving their soaking liquid. Choose a flameproof casserole or heavy-based saucepan large enough to hold the meat in a single layer. Place over medium–high heat, add 1 tablespoon of the olive oil and sear the lamb, turning to brown it evenly on all sides. Remove the meat and set aside.

Reduce the heat to medium and add the remaining tablespoon of oil, along with the onion. Season with salt and pepper and sauté for 2 minutes or until soft. Add the garlic, ginger, turmeric and cinnamon, together with the rest of the spice mix, and keep cooking, stirring constantly so the spices don't burn, for about 5 minutes or until the garlic, ginger and turmeric have softened and the spices are fragrant.

Return the seared meat to the pan, then add the carrots, honey and reserved prune-soaking liquid, stirring the base of the pan to deglaze. Pour in the tomatoes and bring to the boil, then add the orange zest, prunes and bay leaf and simmer for 5 minutes. Add enough stock or water to cover, bring back to the boil, then reduce to a very low simmer (use a simmer mat, if you have one). Cover with a circle of baking paper, pressing it directly onto the surface of the tagine, then cover with a lid and cook for 1½–2 hours or until the meat is very tender, stirring occasionally to make sure nothing sticks to the pan and burns.

Scatter the parsley, almonds and preserved lemon over the tagine and serve with couscous or freekeh (or any other cooked grain of your choice).

KRISTEN'S BAKED RICOTTA

This is the traditional southern Italian way to bake ricotta, called *ricotta infornata*, which cheese-maker Kristen introduced us to. As the ricotta takes time to drain and become firm, this recipe needs to be started several days in advance. If you like, you can add grapes, olives or figs to the ricotta after you have turned the oven down, to let the flavours cook in for that extra 10 minutes.

Alternatively, you can serve baked ricotta as a dessert, topped with pistachios and a drizzle of honey.

PREPARATION TIME
10 minutes, plus 3–4 days draining

COOKING TIME
30 minutes

SERVES 8

1 kg (2 lb 4 oz) ricotta
olive oil, for drizzling
1 rosemary sprig, leaves only
a few thyme sprigs, leaves only
1 tablespoon finely grated orange zest

Place your ricotta in a colander or sieve lined with muslin (cheesecloth) and set over a bowl. Cover and leave in the fridge to drain for 3–4 days, depending on how firm you want the baked ricotta to be.

Preheat the oven to 220°C (425°F/gas mark 7) and line a baking tray with baking paper.

Gently turn out the ricotta onto the prepared baking tray. Drizzle with olive oil and season with salt and pepper, rubbing the ricotta all over and making sure it is totally covered with oil.

Bake the ricotta for 10–15 minutes or until it has turned a lovely golden colour.

Take the ricotta out of the oven and turn the oven down to 100°C (200°F/gas mark ½). Sprinkle the ricotta with the rosemary and thyme leaves and the orange zest, then return it to the oven and bake for a further 10 minutes.

Transfer to a board and serve while still warm.

PREPARATION TIME
20 minutes,
plus 15 minutes
heat-processing

STORAGE
up to 2 years

MAKES
5 × 500 ml
(17 fl oz/2 cup) jars

PICKLED CUMQUATS

These were among the first pickles we ever made. Our neighbour at the time had three huge cumquat trees in his front yard, so we knocked on his door one day and asked what he did with them all. He gave us a list of the ways his family preserved their harvest of cumquats: as marmalade and syrup, and in salt, adding that the salted ones were very good for sore throats.

These cumquats were first inspired by a Stephanie Alexander recipe, though we add cumin and peppercorns to ours. They're great in a stuffing for roast chicken, or added to Moroccan-style stews. They're also awesome with stinky cheese.

At the cafe we often toss thinly sliced pickled cumquats through salads (see page 42) and use the brine to make a dressing as well – just add some extra virgin olive oil.

1 litre (35 fl oz/4 cups) white wine vinegar
500 g (1 lb 2 oz) caster (superfine) sugar
1 teaspoon black peppercorns
2 teaspoons cumin seeds
1.5 kg (3 lb 5 oz) cumquats
5 cinnamon sticks
5 cloves

Make a brine by putting the vinegar, sugar and 500 ml (17 fl oz/2 cups) of water into a non-reactive saucepan over low heat. Stir to dissolve the sugar, then add the peppercorns and cumin seeds. Increase the heat and bring to the boil. Turn off the heat and let the brine sit for about 15 minutes to allow the flavours to develop.

Meanwhile, sterilise your jars (see page 250).

Remove any stems from the cumquats. Bring the brine back to a simmer and, working in batches, slip the cumquats into the brine for a few minutes to soften them slightly – when their skins turn glossy, they're ready. Use a slotted spoon to scoop them out, then set aside in a bowl.

When the jars are cool enough to handle, use small tongs or clean hands to carefully pack the cumquats into the jars, adding a cinnamon stick and a clove to each jar. You want to pack as many cumquats into each jar as possible without bursting the skins (see page 252 for more on packing techniques).

Carefully fill the jars with the hot brine until the cumquats are completely covered. Remove any air bubbles by gently tapping each jar on the work surface and sliding a butter knife or chopstick around the inside to release any hidden air pockets. You may need to add more brine or cumquats after doing this (the liquid should reach about 1 cm/½ in from the top of the jar). Wipe the rims of the jars with paper towel and seal.

Heat-process (see page 255) for 15 minutes, then store in a cool, dark place. Let the cumquats sit for at least a month before using. Once a jar is opened, store in the fridge and use within 6 months.

PICCALILLI

This English pickle is the perfect thing to take to a picnic. We also add it to ham and cheese sandwiches, and spoon some onto our ploughman's plates (see page 160).

You can use any vegetables you have on hand for this. We make seasonal variations, depending on what's available. Radish, zucchini (courgettes), choko (chayote), white cabbage, daikon, thinly sliced brussels sprouts, green chillies and onion are all great to use – you need a kilo of vegetables all up.

PREPARATION TIME
45 minutes

COOKING TIME
10 minutes, plus 10 minutes heat-processing

STORAGE
up to 12 months

MAKES
4 x 300 ml (10½ fl oz) jars

350 g (12 oz) cauliflower (about ¼ medium cauliflower), cut into small florets
150 g (5½ oz) carrot (about 1 medium–large carrot), thinly sliced
250 g (9 oz) fennel (about ¼ large or 1 small fennel bulb), thinly sliced
250 g (9 oz) green beans, cut into thirds
4 cloves
1 teaspoon ground fenugreek
1 teaspoon black peppercorns
2 tablespoons brown mustard seeds
250 ml (9 fl oz/1 cup) white wine vinegar
2 tablespoons cornflour (cornstarch)
2 teaspoons salt
½ teaspoon ground turmeric
100 g (3½ oz) caster (superfine) sugar

Bring a large saucepan of salted water to the boil. Add the cauliflower florets and blanch for 1 minute, then drain and refresh under cold running water. Mix the cauliflower and all the other vegetables together.

Grind the cloves, fenugreek seeds, peppercorns and half of the mustard seeds into a fine powder using a spice grinder.

Next, sterilise your jars (see page 250).

For the piccalilli base, combine the vinegar with 250 ml (9 fl oz/1 cup) of water in a non-reactive saucepan. In a large heatproof bowl, mix the cornflour, salt and turmeric with the ground spices and the remaining mustard seeds, then stir in 60 ml (2 fl oz/¼ cup) of the vinegar mixture to make a smooth paste. Add the sugar to the remaining vinegar mixture, then place over medium heat and stir until the sugar has dissolved. Slowly pour the hot brine into the cornflour paste, whisking as you go, to make a smooth, thick sauce. Add the vegetables and gently stir through until they are evenly coated with the sauce.

Pack the hot piccalilli into the hot jars, seal and heat-process (see page 255) for 10 minutes. Store the jars in a cool, dark place for at least a month before using. Unopened jars of piccalilli will keep for up to 12 months. Once opened, refrigerate and use within 3 months.

PREPARATION TIME
10 minutes

COOKING TIME
3–4 hours

STORAGE
up to 2 weeks

MAKES
about 400 ml
(14 fl oz)

WHEY CARAMEL

As well as making fresh cheeses for Cornersmith, Kristen provides us with lots of whey, a by-product of cheese-making. We often share ideas on how to avoid waste and make good use of what we have on hand, so now we make this whey caramel, bake whey into our cakes and muffins, use it as a marinade for meat and in salad dressings (see page 260).

If you make your own labneh (see page 37) or cheese, this is a delicious way to use up the left-over whey. With a lovely semi-sweet, malty flavour, it's great with ice cream, in milkshakes, or poured over hearty winter puddings.

1 litre (35 fl oz/4 cups) whey
250 g (9 oz) caster (superfine) sugar

Pour the whey through a fine sieve into a heavy-based saucepan. Add the sugar and bring it slowly to the boil, stirring to dissolve the sugar.

Turn down the heat as low as possible (use a simmer mat, if you have one) and let it simmer without a lid for about 3–4 hours, stirring regularly, until you have a thick, golden caramel. Keep an eye on it, and once it starts getting a caramel colour, stay with it and stir frequently – you don't want the caramel to get too dark, or it will be too hard when cool.

As soon as you're happy with the colour and consistency of your caramel, take it off the heat straightaway. Let it cool down for a couple of minutes before carefully pouring it into a clean glass jar (if it's too hot when pouring, the glass may shatter). Cool completely, then store in the fridge for up to 2 weeks.

If you want a runnier caramel for pouring over desserts, sit the jar in a saucepan of hot water for around 10 minutes, stirring it every now and then.

PEARS POACHED IN RED WINE

PREPARATION TIME
10 minutes

COOKING TIME
30 minutes

STORAGE
up to 5 days

SERVES 6–8

An all-time favourite, these poached pears are very versatile. And they absorb the flavours of the syrup really well, so they just get better and better as they sit. At Cornersmith we serve them for breakfast, but they're a great thing to have in the fridge, either as the starting point for an easy dessert, or for adding to muesli or yoghurt. They go really well with lemon myrtle yoghurt – just stir ¼ teaspoon of ground lemon myrtle through 250 g (9 oz) of natural yoghurt.

This amount of poaching liquid is enough for about 6–8 pears (you'll want more!). If you're organised enough, you can make the poaching liquid the day before and let it sit overnight in the fridge to deepen its flavour.

1 litre (35 fl oz/4 cups) red wine
500 g (1 lb 2 oz) caster (superfine) sugar
2 star anise
2 bay leaves
1 small rosemary sprig
1 thyme sprig
3 strips of orange zest
3 strips of lemon zest
6–8 just-ripe pears – beurre bosc work well
juice of 1 lemon

Choose a non-reactive saucepan that will just hold the pears snugly. Pour in the wine and add the sugar, star anise, bay leaves, rosemary, thyme and orange and lemon zest. Bring to the boil, then simmer for 5–10 minutes.

Meanwhile, peel the pears, squeezing lemon juice over them as they're done to stop them discolouring.

Add the pears to the pan and cover with a circle of baking paper, pressing it directly onto the surface of the liquid. Simmer for 15–20 minutes or until the pears are cooked – you should be able to easily insert the tip of a knife into the centre of the fruit. Remove from the heat and leave the pears to cool in the poaching liquid.

Store the pears covered in the poaching liquid, in the fridge, for up to 5 days. If you like, you can simmer some of the poaching liquid to reduce it to a syrup that will coat the pears for serving.

PREPARATION TIME
20 minutes

COOKING TIME
1 hour

MAKES
about 24

COCOA & WATTLESEED MERINGUE STICKS

These add a crunchy texture and beautiful flavour to cakes, desserts and ice cream. If you want more free-form meringues, just spread the uncooked meringue onto the lined baking trays, sprinkle with the topping and then break into irregular pieces after baking.

**100 g (3½ oz) egg whites
   (from about 3 free-range eggs)
100 g (3½ oz) caster (superfine) sugar
50 g (1¾ oz) icing (confectioners') sugar, sifted
20 g (¾ oz) dutch-processed cocoa powder, sifted,
   plus extra for dusting
ground wattleseed, cocoa nibs or chopped nuts,
   for sprinkling**

Preheat the oven to 120°C (235°F/gas mark ½) and line two baking trays with baking paper.

Using a stand mixer fitted with a whisk attachment or hand-held electric beaters, whisk the egg whites until soft peaks form. Gradually add the caster sugar and keep whisking until the meringue is firm and glossy.

Using a spatula, gently fold through the icing sugar and cocoa powder.

Fit a piping (icing) bag with a 1 cm (½ in) nozzle and fill with the meringue. Pipe the meringue onto the prepared baking trays in lines, swirls or any other shape you like. Dust with cocoa powder and sprinkle over some wattleseed.

Bake the meringue for 1 hour or until completely dry.

FRANCA'S DARK CHOCOLATE TART

This tart is a serious dessert on its own, but if you really want to show off, serve it with the poached pears from page 241 and the meringue sticks opposite. If you have any sweet pastry left over from lining the tart tin, use it to make some jam triangles (see page 199).

1 quantity sweet pastry (see page 57)
225 g (8 oz) dark (70% cocoa) chocolate, roughly chopped
90 g (3¼ oz) unsalted butter, cut into cubes
2 free-range eggs, lightly beaten
80 ml (2½ fl oz/⅓ cup) pouring cream
50 g (1¾ oz) caster (superfine) sugar
dutch-processed cocoa powder, for dusting
pears poached in red wine (see page 241), to serve
cocoa and wattleseed meringue sticks (see opposite), to serve

PREPARATION TIME
40 minutes, plus 30 minutes resting

COOKING TIME
50 minutes

MAKES
1 x 20 cm (8 in) tart

Prepare the sweet pastry case as instructed on page 57. After blind-baking, remove it from the oven and leave to cool on a wire rack. Reduce the oven temperature to 170°C (325°F/gas mark 3).

Put the chocolate and butter into a heatproof bowl and set over a saucepan of simmering water, ensuring the base of the bowl isn't touching the water. Stir until completely melted, then remove from the heat and leave to cool for 5 minutes.

In another bowl, whisk together the eggs, cream and sugar until smooth, then add the melted chocolate mixture and whisk until combined. Pour into the cooled pastry case and bake for 20–25 minutes or until the edges are slightly puffed but the centre still wobbles slightly when the tin is gently shaken.

Leave the tart to cool in its tin on a wire rack. Dust with cocoa powder and top with poached pear halves and meringue sticks to serve.

PRESERVING

PRESERVING

One of the things we want to do with this book is to encourage you to have a go at making your own pickles, sauces, relishes, ferments, jams and marmalades.

The idea is to preserve fruit and vegetables when they are abundant and at the height of their season, so they can be safely stored and eaten later. But you can't just put fruit and vegetables into jars and hope for the best – you have to create a hostile, anaerobic (oxygen-free) environment for harmful micro-organisms, to prevent your preserves from spoiling. This is done with the help of preserving agents (sugar, salt, vinegar and alcohol), or special techniques such as salting, fermenting and drying; heat may also be used to kill off any bacteria already present.

People have been preserving food at home for centuries. All it takes is practice, time and patience. The best advice we can give you is not to be afraid – and to relax and have fun. Once you've got your head around the different processes, preserving is easy, rewarding, creative and sustainable.

EQUIPMENT

You don't need much in the way of equipment to start preserving at home. In our workshops we suggest starting with what you have in your kitchen. Then, once you're feeling more confident, you can buy a few more specialised items to help make things easier.

PANS
For making jams, marmalade, chutneys and relishes, the type of pan you use is important. For years we made do with a regular medium-sized saucepan, and for small batches of up to 2 kg (4 lb 8 oz) it worked fine, but as soon as we tried to increase the batch size, our jam wouldn't set and our chutneys wouldn't thicken. It wasn't until we splurged on a proper jam pan that we understood what a difference the right pan makes.

Essentially, you need a wide, fairly shallow pan to give a large surface area for even cooking and evaporation: if your pan is too deep, the jam or chutney at the bottom of the pan will cook more quickly than the rest, resulting in jam that won't set and chutney that won't thicken evenly.

A jam pan or preserving pan with tapered sides is ideal, of course, but any wide, heavy-based, shallow stainless-steel saucepan or enamelled cast-iron casserole is fine to start with.

Avoid aluminium pans, as they taint any acidic ingredients (fruit, citrus juices, vinegar, etc) cooked in them. And while copper pans are traditionally used for making jam and have excellent heat-conducting properties, they shouldn't be used for chutney, as the metal reacts to vinegar-based preserves.

If you get bitten by the preserving bug, buy a good-quality jam pan that you'll be able to pass down to the next generation.

CLAMPS
These are a lifesaver. You use them to safely transfer hot sterilised jars from the oven to your benchtop, and to remove filled jars from the heat-processing pan.

You can get by with oven mitts and thick cloths in the short term, but clamps are inexpensive to buy and will spare you many burnt arms and hands. Avoid the cheap wire ones, as they won't last and don't always have the best grip. Try to find the sturdier sort, made of stainless steel with a rubber grip.

FUNNELS
A wide-mouthed funnel guides your chutneys and jams into the jars without any spills, saving you time and mess.

If you're keen, invest in a range of different-sized funnels, so you can easily decant syrups and sauces into bottles, as well as filling jars with jams and chutneys. Otherwise, carefully pour or spoon in your product, then use a clean cloth or paper towel to wipe any spills, drips or stickiness from the rim of the jar or bottle.

JARS

When you're starting out, just use what you've got in the kitchen cupboard. Second-hand jars are fine to re-use, as long as there are no cracks or chips in the glass that could harbour micro-organisms or cause the jar to break when heated. Second-hand metal (but not plastic) lids are OK too, if they are in good condition. Make sure there is no rust, and that the white acid-proof coating inside the lids is intact. Also check that the lids aren't misshapen or dented, as both of these can interfere with the seal.

If you decide to buy new jars, get good-quality ones made of thick glass – we'd recommend going to a kitchen supply shop and buying 20 jars and 40 lids. Cheap jars from discount stores often have thin glass, which tends to become brittle at high temperatures.

STERILISING JARS AND BOTTLES

To sterilise jars or bottles, give them a wash in hot soapy water and a good rinse, then place in a cold oven. Heat the oven to 110°C (225°F/gas mark ½) and, once it has reached temperature, leave the jars in the oven for about 10 minutes or until completely dry, then remove them carefully.

To sterilise the lids, place them in a large saucepan of boiling water for 5 minutes, then drain and dry with clean paper towels or leave them on a wire rack to air dry. Make sure they are completely dry before using.

MAKING JAM AND MARMALADE

PREPARING AND COOKING THE FRUIT

Larger pieces of fruit will make a chunkier jam; smaller pieces will cook more quickly and give a smoother consistency.

Put your fruit into a saucepan, with the required amount of water and any herbs or spices you are using. Cook over low heat until the fruit is very soft before adding the sugar. If the fruit in your jam or the skin in your marmalade is still firm, once you add sugar it will candy – and a hard piece of fruit can ruin a jam.

Next add any lemon or lime juice or zest. As citrus fruit contains high levels of pectin and acid (see opposite), adding these now will also help your jam to set.

ADDING THE SUGAR

Next, add the sugar, stirring to dissolve it completely. Sugar is the main preserving agent in jam and marmalade, with high levels of sugar keeping micro-organisms at bay. We have experimented with all kinds of sugar, but have found that caster (superfine) sugar gives the best results. Don't play around with reducing sugar levels until you've mastered jam-making, as it will affect the set and shelf life.

TESTING FOR 'SETTING POINT'

Turn up the heat and boil your jam or marmalade rapidly, stirring occasionally, until it reaches 'setting point' – the two words that always seem to spread panic in our jam workshops! There are many ways to test for setting point, but we find the easiest method is to put several small saucers in the freezer before you start. Once the sugar is in the pan and your jam has been bubbling away for 20 minutes (or 15 minutes for marmalade), get one of the saucers out of the freezer and drop a small spoonful onto it. Let it sit for a minute or so, then run your finger through it: if your finger leaves a clear line that stays put (see the picture on page 15), your jam or marmalade has reached setting point. You can test multiple times, but once you get close to your jam being ready, take it off the heat while you test, as it's a very fine line between nicely set and over-cooked jam.

Other signs that your jam is ready include a thick texture, glossy surface and bubbles that are heavy and slow, unlike the fast bubbles at the beginning of cooking. Keep in mind that a brightly coloured, fruity-tasting, soft-set jam is a better option than a hard-set, dark over-cooked and lifeless jam. (Remember too that if you increase the batch size, you'll also need to increase the cooking time. Only attempt a double batch if you have the right pan, though; otherwise you're better off doing two batches one after the other.)

As soon as setting point is reached, turn off the heat. If any 'scum' has formed on the surface of the jam, either stir it in or remove it with a slotted spoon – it's perfectly harmless, but some people prefer to skim it off for aesthetic reasons.

AND IF THINGS DON'T GO TO PLAN...
If your jam or marmalade refuses to cooperate, don't throw it away. Unset jam is great on ice cream, in smoothies or in ice blocks (see page 63). Over-cooked jam can be used in marinades and glazes: we often save a jar of over-cooked jam to use as the base of our glaze for the Christmas ham.

FILLING AND STORING THE JARS
Carefully pour the hot jam into hot sterilised jars (see opposite), leaving a 5 mm (¼ in) gap at the top of the jar. Wipe the rims of the jars with paper towel or a clean damp cloth and seal immediately. Store unopened jars of jam and marmalade in a cool, dark place; once opened, they should be kept in the fridge and used within a few months. The actual storage time will vary, depending on the sugar content, but this detailed information is given for each recipe. If you want to make a bigger batch and keep it for longer, then heat-process (see page 255) your jars of jam or marmalade before storing them.

SETTING POINT
To successfully 'set' your jam, the right levels of pectin, acid, heat and sugar all have to come together, so understanding the pectin and acid levels in your produce is important.

PECTIN
Found naturally in fruit and vegetables, at varying levels, pectin helps your jam or marmalade to set. The most successful jams are made with high-pectin fruits, such as quince and apple (see page 128), but experimenting with combinations of low- and high-pectin fruits, as in peach and lime jam (see page 73), also gives good results.

High pectin: all citrus fruit, grapes, green apples, plums, quinces
Medium pectin: blackberries, blueberries, raspberries, mulberries, red apples, passionfruit
Low pectin: apricots, cherries, figs, nectarines, peaches, pears, pineapple, strawberries

You can also buy powdered pectin, or special 'jam sugar' with pectin added, and these are worth trying if you want a well-set jam; they can be rather temperamental, however, so follow the instructions on the packet.

ACID
Like pectin, acid is found in varying amounts in all fruit. Acidity helps to draw the pectin out of the fruit, and keeps your jam's flavour and colour clear and bright. So if you are making a jam with low-acid fruit, you should pair it with a fruit that is high in acid, or the juice of a lemon.

High acid: all citrus fruit, blueberries, green apples, mulberries
Medium acid: plums, raspberries
Low acid: apricots, cherries, figs, peaches, pears, quince, red apples

PICKLING

Alex's love for pickling started the Cornersmith adventure, and it has become our signature. You'll never get sick of having a pantry full of home-made pickled vegetables for salads, burgers, sandwiches, cheese plates, or just to eat straight from the jar.

The formula for all pickles is basically the same, with variations depending on the type of vinegar, the spices and the way you cut your vegetables. This means that once you're comfortable with the process, you can go nuts!

CHOOSING PRODUCE FOR PICKLING
Use firm, tasty produce that's at the height of its season. Anything that's starting to soften or deteriorate is better used up in chutneys and relishes.

SALTING
Produce with a high water content, such as cucumbers, zucchini (courgettes), green tomatoes and chokos (chayote), needs to be salted before you start pickling – the salt draws out excess moisture and helps keep your pickles crunchy. It's important to use pure salt, with no iodine or anti-caking agents that can make your brine cloudy.

Sliced pickles, also known as 'bread and butter' pickles, should be salted for a few hours, while whole vegetables like baby cucumbers or zucchini (courgettes) need to be salted overnight. After salting, discard the liquid that has been drawn out of the vegetables. You shouldn't need to rinse the vegetables, but if you've been heavy-handed with the salting, by all means give them a quick rinse and then drain well.

MAKING A BRINE
The ratio we use to make our brine is 4 parts vinegar and 2 parts water to 1 part sugar (4:2:1), plus salt to taste. Put the vinegar, water, sugar and salt (if your vegetables have already been salted, you can leave the salt out) into a non-reactive saucepan, stirring to dissolve the sugar. Bring to the boil and let it simmer for a few minutes, then turn off the heat.

The better quality your vinegar, the better your pickles will be. You don't need to buy the most expensive vinegar, but try to find mid-range white and red wine vinegars you can buy in larger quantities. Apple cider vinegar is lovely for pickling fruit. Match the vinegar with the produce – for example, red wine vinegar with beetroot, or white wine vinegar with bread and butter pickles. Note that vinegar for pickling needs to have an acidity of 5% or higher – this should be indicated on the label.

The 4:2:1 ratio makes a well-balanced brine. You can reduce or increase the sugar according to your taste, but don't mess with the vinegar levels.

PACKING PICKLES INTO JARS
We usually 'cold-pack' our pickles, packing the raw vegetables and spices directly into cooled sterilised jars (see page 250) to help maintain their colour and crunch. Occasionally we'll give hard vegetables, such as whole baby beetroot or brussels sprouts, a quick blanch first.

Packing fruit or vegetables perfectly into jars takes practice. You want to get in as much as possible, but without squashing or bruising them, or bursting their skins, so you need a firm hand but a gentle touch. Aim to fill the jars to just below the rim, leaving enough room for the vegetables to be completely covered in brine without them touching the lid.

Slowly pour the hot brine over the vegetables, making sure they're completely submerged (anything left uncovered will discolour and deteriorate, and could potentially go mouldy). It's important to get rid of any air bubbles from the jars before sealing them or the pickles may spoil, because the oxygen in the bubbles enables micro-organisms to thrive. To do this, gently tap each jar on the work surface and slide a clean butter knife or chopstick around the inside of the jar to release any hidden air pockets – you will see bubbles being released from in between the pickles. You may need to add more vegetables or

brine afterwards. There needs to be a gap of 5 mm–1.5 cm (¼–⅝ in) between the brine and the lid – this is called 'headspace', and it allows the vegetables to expand as they absorb the brine. Keep in mind that smaller and sliced vegetables, such as the fennel on page 220, will absorb less brine than larger ones like the whole cumquats on page 234, so adjust the headspace accordingly.

STORAGE

Wipe the rims of the jars with paper towel or a clean cloth, then put the lids on. If you are planning on storing your pickles for an extended amount of time, we suggest you heat-process them. Pickles that have been heat-processed and stored correctly – in a cool, dark place – will last for up to 2 years unopened. Make sure you stick to any recommended storage times given in specific recipes. If you don't want to heat-process your pickles, you'll need to store them in the fridge and use them up within a month.

The advantage of heat-processing is that pickles get better over time. Whole pickles need to sit in their jars for at least 6 weeks before use, but will taste even better after 6 months. Sliced pickles are ready after 2 weeks and are best eaten within 6 months, before their texture starts to deteriorate. Once opened, all pickles should be refrigerated.

HEAT-PROCESSING

Also called water bathing or canning, this process uses heat to stop the growth of bacteria and generate pressure inside the preserving jar or bottle, which forces out any oxygen to create an uninhabitable environment for micro-organisms. Treating your preserves in this way has two benefits: it lengthens their shelf life, and it ensures the jars or bottles are sealed correctly. Opinions differ on when heat-processing is necessary, but at Cornersmith we encourage our students to heat-process any cold-packed preserves, pickles and bottled fruit – as well as large batches of chutneys and jams that will be stored for some time. Here's how it's done.

Get the biggest pan you have, such as a stockpot – the taller, the better – and put it on the stovetop. Lay a folded tea towel in the bottom of the pan, then sit your jars on the tea towel, taking care not to cram them in and keeping them clear of the sides of the pan. (All these measures are to stop the jars from wobbling around and cracking as the water boils.) Roughly match the water temperature to the temperature of the jars (to help prevent breakages from thermal shock), then pour in enough water to cover the jars, either completely or at least until three-quarters submerged. Bring to the boil over medium heat. The heat-processing times given in the recipes start from boiling point, and will generally be 10–15 minutes for jars or bottles up to 500 ml (17 fl oz/2 cup) capacity, or 20 minutes for larger capacities.

You may expect one or two breakages when you're starting out – the worst that can happen is that the remaining jars will swim in pickles or jammy water for the rest of the processing time. Just keep going, then take the surviving jars out at the end and give them a wipe down. If they all break, you have our permission to have a gin and a lie-down!

Once the heat-processing time is up, the lids should be puffed up and convex. Carefully remove the hot jars from the water. If you've bought some clamps (see page 248), now is the time to use them, or you can use oven mitts and a thick cloth to protect your hands. Line your jars up on the bench and let them sit overnight. As they cool, a vacuum will form inside each jar and suck down the lid, sealing them securely. In the morning, the lids should be concave: either get down to eye level with the top of the jar to check for the telltale dip in the lid, or lay a pencil across each lid to show the cavity below it. If you have concerns about the seal of any of your jars (sometimes a couple of jars fail to seal correctly), store them in the fridge and use their contents within a few weeks.

MAKING CHUTNEYS AND RELISHES

These are a great way of using up seasonal gluts of vegetables and fruit. And a cupboard full of relishes, chutneys and sauces can turn an average weeknight dinner into something special. The chutneys we make at Cornersmith are thick, rich and spice-driven, with a long cooking time, while the relishes are light, fresh and focused on maintaining the colour, texture and flavour of the produce.

PREPARING FRUIT AND VEGETABLES
Taste the produce you're working with: if it's a bit average tasting, you might want to amp up the spices to give it a lift; but if you're working with amazing pears or plums, you can focus on emphasising their natural flavour, rather than disguising it with heavy spices. Bumps and bruises are fine, but cut out any mould. Cut your vegetables into similar-sized pieces to ensure even cooking and consistency. Larger-cut vegetables will give a more rustic result.

COOKING CHUTNEYS AND RELISHES
Cooking chutneys and relishes takes time and patience. You want the acidity of the vinegar to cook out and the flavours of the spices and produce to develop.

We tend to start by sautéing the onions with the spices and a small amount of oil. This brings out the sweetness of the onions and the fragrance of the spices, and also avoids the harsh raw onion taste you sometimes get if you just chuck everything in and boil it up. Next we add the vegetables and let them soften slightly before adding the rest of the ingredients.

It's important to match the vinegar you use to the produce: beetroot (beet) relish or a rich fruit chutney would work well with red wine vinegar, while green tomato relish (see page 50) is better with white wine vinegar, to let the colour of the vegetables shine.

When your chutney is ready, it should be thick and glossy, with no puddles of liquid on the surface. If you draw your spoon through the chutney, you should momentarily be able to see the bottom of the pan.

BOTTLING AND STORAGE
Once your chutney is ready, pour it into hot sterilised jars (see page 250), wipe the rims with a clean damp cloth and seal immediately. Chutneys and relishes can be stored unopened for up to 12 months in a cool, dark place. Let them sit in their jars for at least 6 weeks before opening – during this time, the vinegar mellows and the other flavours intensify. Once opened, chutneys and relishes should be kept in the fridge. For extended storage, heat-process (see page 255) your chutneys and relishes.

FERMENTING

Along with salting, fermenting is one of the oldest methods of food preservation. Knowingly or not, most of us regularly consume fermented foods: bread, butter, cheese and salami.

At Cornersmith, we're very lucky to have a resident fermenter. Jaimee is passionate about the benefits of fermented foods, and has generously shared her guide to the process so you can try your hand at fermenting at home:

'My cultural background is Russian, and while it would be nice to have memories of making *kapusta kvashenenya* (sauerkraut) with my *baba* (grandmother), the truth is that she and my mother came to Australia in the 1950s and left their preserving skills on the boat. With the exception of *kvass*, a fermented drink made from rye bread, my family preserved nothing, instead scouring the delis and markets of Sydney in search of the foods they missed. Fortunately, many Russian specialities have counterparts in other cultures, so pickled cabbage from Germany and herrings from Sweden sufficed.

As a result, I inherited the palate of "the old country" but none of the skills, so when Alex and I started to pickle, I was keen to learn how to make the condiments that traditionally accompany a Russian meal. I soon discovered that these were often made by fermentation: preserved not with vinegar but through a process called lacto-fermentation.

During lacto-fermentation, the lactic-acid-producing bacteria (lactobacilli) present on the surface of all fruit and vegetables are encouraged to proliferate in an anaerobic (oxygen-free) environment. Salt is used to inhibit the growth of any harmful bacteria for a few days while the "good" lactobacilli generate enough lactic acid to preserve the fruit and vegetables. Pure salt should always be used, at a ratio of about 20 g (¾ oz) fine salt to 2 kg (4 lb 8 oz) produce.

Not only are the vegetables or fruit preserved, but their digestibility and nutrient content is enhanced. Even better, consuming such foods introduces healthy probiotic bacteria into our gut, which may improve our overall health.

Lacto-fermentation is a very safe method of food preservation. However, as with all food preparation, commonsense and good hygiene practices are needed. Cut away any bruised or perishing parts of your produce; wash and sterilise your jars (see page 250); and keep hands, benches and utensils scrupulously clean. Once you've packed your produce into jars, fermentation should begin in a few days. Here's what you need to keep an eye out for.

TIME

The longer you leave your ferment at room temperature, the more its flavour will develop, and the greater the numbers of probiotic bacteria it will contain. Open your jar after a couple of days and see what you think. Your ferment should smell pungent but not foul, and there may be some bubbles. Fermented vegetables have a sour, somewhat yeasty edge to them: think of sourdough bread, strong cheeses and beer. Depending on the pace of the fermentation and how strong you want the flavour to be, you can leave your jar at room temperature (but out of direct sunlight) for anything from 2 days to 2 weeks before refrigerating – we suggest 2 to 4 days to start with. Trust your palate and instinct when it comes to deciding whether your ferment is ready to be moved to the fridge. Your vegetables or fruit will continue to ferment in the fridge, but at a much slower rate, and will keep well for up to 6 months.

TEMPERATURE

In a hot climate, fermentation will be rapid, so during an Australian summer you'll probably need to place your ferments in the refrigerator after 2 or 3 days. Conversely, in cooler conditions, you may need to wait a week or two for fermentation to take place.

SPILLAGE

As fermentation occurs, you may find that the build-up of carbon dioxide, a by-product of the process, forces liquid out of the jar. Just unscrew the lid of your jar and wipe down the rim and sides with paper towel or a clean cloth. If necessary, gently press the vegetables or fruit to re-submerge in the liquid before replacing the lid.

SAFETY

Once fermentation is underway, the environment in the jar is hostile to harmful bacteria, so relax! Very rarely does anything go wrong. However, if any black mould develops on your ferment, throw the contents of that jar away. If a little white mould is visible on the surface, carefully scoop it off and check underneath: the rest of the ferment might well be fine.

Always trust your instincts, though, especially when you first start fermenting – and if something doesn't smell or taste right, discard it.

An unexpected bonus of making fermented foods is that they help to re-build our connection with food, for they are dependent on us and demand our attention. Some trial and error is involved, teaching us to go with the flow. In my classes I joke that fermenting is not for commitment-phobes – but with time and care you will be well rewarded.'

RECIPE BASICS

The recipes in this book should be used as a guideline. The way we work at Cornersmith is to use what's available and in season, which means we're always open to interchanging produce in our dishes and experimenting with other vegetables, fruits and herbs. What we serve is determined by the weather, the seasons, what Shane our vegetable supplier brings us and what we've traded that week, so we have to be flexible. We encourage you to get out of the supermarket, go to farmers' markets and fruit and veg shops, and to plan your cooking around what you find there. If the specific ingredients in a recipe aren't available or you don't like the look of them, try something else instead.

HERBS

We use a lot of seasonal herbs in our dishes at Cornersmith. They add colour, texture and flavour. Be adventurous with your choices – there's a huge variety out there. Make sure you wash and dry them well, and add the more delicate herbs, such as dill and chervil, to dishes just before serving.

We prefer to tear the leaves of softer herbs, rather than cut them – it's quick and easy, and mint and basil in particular discolour less when treated this way. Wrapped in a damp tea towel and sealed in a plastic bag in the vegetable drawer of your fridge, most herbs should keep well for up to a week.

SALT AND PEPPER

Look for a pure salt with no additives (anti-caking agents or extra iodine) and freshly ground black pepper. The amounts of salt given in the recipes in this book are based on fine salt, not rock salt or salt flakes.

DRESSINGS, VINEGARS AND OILS

Salad dressings are an artform in themselves, and they can transform the simplest of ingredients into something extraordinary.

Our approach to making dressings at Cornersmith is a reflection of our food philosophy. We try not to throw anything usable away, and this includes the by-products of the pickling, fermenting and cheese-making processes: the brine at the bottom of the pickle jar, the juice at the end of the kimchi pot, and the whey left after making cheese. These are so full of flavour that it's a shame to pour them down the sink – and, happily, they all make a great base for a salad dressing.

We also recommend a good-quality white or red wine vinegar and maybe another more mellow or aged one – we often use an aged apple balsamic, or an aged sherry vinegar is also delicious.

For the 'oily' element of your dressing, you need a good extra virgin olive oil and a high-quality vegetable oil, such as grapeseed or sunflower. We tend to mix these two oils, as olive oil can be overpowering and mask the other, more subtle flavours in the dressing.

We also like playing around with dairy in our salad dressings, mainly using whey or buttermilk. Yoghurt and kefir are other options if you want to experiment.

To balance out the acidity, we add a small amount of sweetness to our dressings, often in the form of one of our own jams or marmalades, or our rooftop honey, although a pinch of sugar works too.

Start with a ratio of 1 part acid (pickling or fermenting liquid, whey, vinegar, etc) to 2 parts oil. Combine these in a screw-top jar with your choice of flavourings, such as mustard, herbs or spices, and season with salt and pepper. Put on the lid and shake well to emulsify, then taste and adjust. Feel free to vary these elements to find the right balance that works for you.

TOASTING SEEDS AND NUTS

We use a lot of toasted seeds and nuts in our salads. The toasting process is so quick and easy, yet it brings so much more flavour and texture to your dishes. If you are toasting more than one variety, you'll need to do them separately, as they all have different toasting times.

Preheat the oven to 170°C (325°F/gas mark 3). Spread the seeds or nuts onto a baking tray. Set a timer for 3 minutes and then move the nuts or seeds around when it goes off, so they brown evenly. Repeat until golden brown: for almonds, hazelnuts and walnuts, this will take about 8–10 minutes. To see if they are done, cut one open and check that it is golden brown right through. Sunflower, sesame and pumpkin seeds normally take less time, about 5–7 minutes.

SPROUTING PULSES

We're very happy to have Amanda Roberts supply us with sprouts. Here are her tips on how to get sprouting at home:

'Sprouted pulses, seeds and grains are like little power packs of nutrition. A great source of vitamins and protein, they come with their own enzymes, making them easy for the body to digest. Sprouts add texture, colour and flavour to salads and sandwiches, soups and other warm dishes (just make sure you only heat them gently, to preserve their goodness).

Growing your own provides a fresh, clean, living food available throughout the seasons. This simple method requires no special equipment and is suitable for chickpeas, whole lentils, mung beans, black-eyed beans and green peas. As the growing times for all these are similar, a combination of them can be sprouted in one container.

It's best to use organic pulses for sprouting. Place in a deep bowl, cover with cold water and leave to soak for about 8–10 hours, then drain in a sieve or colander. Rinse under the cold tap until the water runs clear and drain very well. Place the sieve or colander over a bowl and cover with a light cloth or tea towel to protect from dust and insects, then leave at room temperature, away from direct sunlight, to germinate. Repeat the rinsing and draining twice daily for 2–3 days.

Your sprouts are ready to eat as soon as the shoot is visible, but you can grow them as short or as long as you like. When you're happy with them, store in a sealed container in the fridge and you'll have fresh sprouts for the week.'

POACHING EGGS

The only eggs we do at Cornersmith are poached eggs, and we match them with a variety of sides and relishes.

Eggs for poaching need to be the freshest possible, and we always use genuinely free-range eggs. Bear in mind that the quality of eggs varies throughout the year, as chooks are very sensitive to changes of temperature, humidity and feed. We find we get much better results with refrigerated eggs.

If you are a beginner, poach one egg at a time, so you can focus on getting each egg nicely shaped and cooked. Fill a large saucepan with water to a depth of 8–10 cm (3¼–4 in). Bring to the boil over medium–high heat, then add 2–3 teaspoons of white vinegar and bring back to the boil. Reduce the heat to low–medium – the water should be just simmering.

Crack an egg onto a saucer or into a ramekin. Stir the simmering water in one direction to create a swirl – this will give your poached eggs a nice shape. As close to the surface of the water as possible, slide the egg from its saucer or ramekin into the centre of the swirl and cook for 2–3 minutes, or until set but still soft to the touch.

Using a slotted spoon, carefully lift out the egg and drain on a plate lined with paper towel. Use the slotted spoon to skim any foam and impurities from the water, then repeat with however many eggs you want to poach.

To reheat your poached eggs, bring a clean pan of water to the boil, then take off the heat. Add the eggs and let them sit in the hot water for 1 minute. Remove and drain, then serve straightaway.

ABOUT CORNERSMITH

We are constantly growing and learning from the people involved with the business. Our staff share our passion for local, seasonal food, and a firm belief in what we are trying to do at Cornersmith. We work very closely with our suppliers, and what we do is often dictated or inspired by them.

Without these people, Cornersmith wouldn't be what it is today. They play a huge part in our business, and have been invaluable in the making of this book.

Sabine Spindler

Sabine is our main chef at the cafe; she teaches cooking classes at the picklery, and has made this cookbook with us.

Alex and Sabine first met when they were both working in an abandoned bowling-club kitchen one day a week. Alex was trying her luck at pickling on a bigger scale, and Sabine was busy making soups and stocks for our friends at Feather and Bone. Long days spent in a hot kitchen bond people quickly. Exhaustion, dubious jokes and lunches eaten in the old pokies room led to lots of conversations, and the discovery of a shared vision and very similar ideas when it came to food.

Sabine came on board in February 2013, and has taken Cornersmith into another league. She is immensely creative and resourceful, hardworking, unjustly humble and an absolute pleasure to work with. Her attention to detail and her passion for quality is quite something, and she is completely committed to making the very best, most delicious, good-looking food. We love her! This book is hers as much as it is ours. We can't thank her enough.

Jaimee Edwards

Jaimee is the other half of the Cornersmith pickling and preserving duo. She makes all of our ferments, researches new preserves and tests recipes. Jaimee also teaches preserving and fermenting at the picklery, and has contributed many of her recipes to this book.

Alex and Jaimee met when they were both at home with small children. Much in need of a project bigger than play-dough, they started having weekly kitchen dates, where they'd discuss the issues surrounding modern food production (food miles, factory farming, labelling, preservatives, etc) while teaching themselves how to make food from scratch. They both discovered a love of preserving, which kick-started Cornersmith's journey.

Jaimee has been a huge part of Cornersmith, right from the planning stages – she even painted the ceiling of the cafe at midnight two days before we opened! Since then, she has spent countless hours stirring vats of chutney and chopping cabbage. A creative and inspiring teacher and cook, she keeps the picklery well stocked with delicious products and dirty jokes.

Kristen Allan

Kristen supplies us with her beautiful cheeses: labneh, buttermilk ricotta, fetta, yoghurt and quark. She also teaches cheese-making at the picklery and has given us a few of her recipes for this book.

Kristen is one of a kind, and has been a true inspiration for us, our menu, and our way of working. We met her when she catered our wedding. I think it was love at first sight! She worked on the floor at the cafe in the early days, and pickled with us all night long when stocks were low. Being a seasoned restaurant worker, she is often our guide, holding our hands through the many stresses of hospitality. She has become an integral part of Cornersmith.

Shane Roberts
Shane is our much-loved providore. He's like an encyclopedia of all things fruit and vegetable. In the early days of Cornersmith, when we were hunting for small-scale growers, his name kept coming up. And when Alex finally called him, we knew we'd found our man. Plus, now we don't have to trek to the markets at 4 a.m. three times a week!

Shane has a great relationship with the growers and brings us stories from their farms. He is committed to seasonality, and always finds the best produce around. We'll give him an idea about what we're imagining for a dish or preserve, and he comes back with something amazing. He also brings treats from the markets for us to taste – pretty chive flowers, local plums, crazy flowering weeds – and gives us tips about where to forage for things close by.

Shane's wife, Amanda Roberts, is a sprout-er. She grows sprouts for us, and has kindly shared her sprouting tips (see page 261).

Feather and Bone
Essentially, we designed the menu at Cornersmith to be an extension of the way we eat at home: vegetables, fruit and grains dominate, with a small amount of sustainably and ethically raised meat, eggs and dairy. We always knew that our meat choices would need some careful consideration. With so much legal and ethical uncertainty around 'free-range' labelling, and the complexity of sustainability issues, we had to find the right suppliers. Grant Hilliard and Laura Dalrymple are pioneers when it comes to sourcing meat from sustainably raised and ethically treated animals, and we wholeheartedly respect their first-hand knowledge, commitment and unwavering principles.

Urban Beehive
While we were planning Cornersmith, we'd been reading about rooftop bees in Hong Kong and Melbourne, and so we were determined to find some hives for our own rooftop in Marrickville. Our search led us to Doug Purdie and Vicky Brown of the Urban Beehive, who set up beehives in backyards, community gardens and on rooftops across Sydney, with the aim of helping to protect local bee populations and raise awareness of the importance of bees.

They installed our hives on the garage rooftop, and the bees now produce about 80 litres of honey each year. As this is raw honey, it's unheated, unpasteurised and unprocessed, with a much higher nutritional value. The taste and colour of the honey changes with each harvest, depending on where the bees have been feeding – we even had a neighbour come into the picklery the other day to say they'd had a bumper crop of cucumbers this year because our bees had visited their garden so frequently. The response to the honey, the hives and the bees has been so positive that Doug and Vicky now run Producers' nights at the picklery, covering all things bee- and honey-related.

INDEX

Page numbers in *italics* refer to photographs.

acid, in fruit 251
aioli, preserved lemon 96, 97
almonds
   roasted spiced cauliflower salad 217, *218*
   smoky paprika and rosemary toasted almonds 34, *35*
   toasting 261
apples
   apple and quince jam 128, *129*
   apple cider vinegar 252
   apple, kale, sprouts and seed salad with buttermilk dressing *134*, 135
   apple, leek and goat's curd frittata 132, *133*
   apple sauce with cider 150, *151*
   Maeve's baked apples 180, *181*
   ploughman's plate 160, *161*
   pork chops with apple sauce, fennel and mustard 156, *157*
apricots
   apricot and cardamom compote 118
   apricot and cardamom milkshake 118, *119*
asparagus, in vegetable and chicken soup 24–25, *26–27*

bagel with pulled chicken, miso mayonnaise and garlic chips 28, *29*
baked apples 180, *181*
baked ricotta 232, *233*
beans and preserved lemon mash 222, 223
beetroot
   hot pink turnips *48*, 49
   roasted beetroot and rhubarb salad with fetta 213
bitter lime marmalade *126*, 127

bittersweet tabouleh with radicchio and pomegranate 138, *139*
blackberry jam 124, *125*
bread
   Cornersmith Reuben-style sandwich 210
   naan bread with red cabbage slaw, spiced pork and veal and green tomato relish *88*, 89
bread and butter cucumber pickles *110*, 111, *112–113*, 210
brine, how to make 252
broad beans
   broad beans, meatballs and yoghurt 40, *41*
   spring green salad 18, *19*
   vegetable and chicken soup 24–25, *26–27*
brussels slaw with whey dressing, pomelo, hazelnuts and poached egg *202*, 203
buns, sugar plum 183, *184*
buttermilk dressing with kale, apple, sprouts and seed salad *134*, 135

cabbage
   cabbage, kohlrabi and spring herb slaw with pickled cumquats 42, *43*
   Jaimee's sauerkraut *148*, 149
   red cabbage, pickled corn, chilli and coriander slaw 82, *83*
   red cabbage slaw, spiced pork and veal and green tomato relish with naan bread *88*, 89
cakes
   gingerbread layer cake with rhubarb, ricotta and walnuts 188, *189*
   hazelnut meringue cake with lime curd, peach and mango *120*, 121

canning 255
capsicum with barbecued fish, herb salad and preserved lemon aioli *92*, 93
caramel, whey 238, *239*
cardamom
   cardamom and apricot compote 118
   cardamom and apricot milkshake 118, *119*
carrots
   carrot and orange soup *208*, 209
   carrot jam 200, *201*
   carrot loaf 192, *193*
   fermented carrots 224, *225*
   lamb tagine with prunes and fresh turmeric 228–229, *230*
   piccalilli *236*, 237
   vegetable and chicken soup 24–25, *26–27*
cauliflower
   cauliflower salad *216*, 217, *218*
   piccalilli *236*, 237
chard and wild greens pie 204–205, *206*
cheese
   baked ricotta 232, *233*
   cheesecake *56*, 57
   fetta with roasted beetroot and rhubarb salad 213
   labneh *36*, 37
   ploughman's plate 160, *161*
   Reuben-style sandwich 210
   ricotta and figs on toast with honey and fennel flowers 78, *79*
   ricotta and green tomato salad *22*, 23
   ricotta and roasted eggplant with walnuts and pomegranate *154*, 155
   ricotta cream 187
   wattleseed mascarpone with persimmons *186*, 187
cheesecake *56*, 57

cherry and tomato gazpacho
   90, *91*
chervil, chives, cabbage and
   kohlrabi slaw with pickled
   cumquats 42, *43*
chicken
   bagel with pulled chicken,
      miso mayonnaise and
      garlic chips *28,* 29
   chicken and vegetable
      soup 24–25, *26–27*
chillies
   chilli and fermented
      pineapple sambal
      114, *115*
   chilli jam 54, *55*
   chilli, orange and fennel
      salt *32,* 33
   chilli, pickled corn, red
      cabbage and coriander
      slaw 82, *83*
   chilli with pickled fennel
      220, *221*
   pickled green chillies *44,* 45
chives, chervil, cabbage and
   kohlrabi slaw with pickled
   cumquats 42, *43*
chocolate tart 243, *244*
choko pickles *226,* 227
chutneys
   how to make 256, *257*
   pear, lemon and rosemary
      chutney *162,* 163
   tomato and eggplant
      chutney 108, *109*
cider with apple sauce 150, *151*
citrus-braised fennel *140,* 141
clamps 248, 255
cocoa and wattleseed meringue
   sticks 242, *244–245*
cordial, lemon 68, *69*
coriander
   chilli and fermented
      pineapple sambal
      114, *115*
   coriander, red cabbage,
      pickled corn and chilli
      slaw 82, *83*
corn
   corn, red cabbage, chilli
      and coriander slaw 82, *83*
   corn salsa *166,* 167
corned beef, in Reuben-style
   sandwich 210
Cornersmith mustard *158,* 159
Cornersmith poached egg roll
   66, 67
Cornersmith Reuben-style
   sandwich 210, *211*

Cornersmith toasted muesli
   16, 17
cucumbers, pickled *110,*
   111, *112–113*
cumquats
   pickled 234, *235*
   pickled cumquats with
      kohlrabi, cabbage and
      spring herb slaw 42, *43*
custard, vanilla 182

dark chocolate tart 243, *244*
dilly beans *116,* 117
dip, white bean and
   preserved lemon *222,* 223
dressings 260

eggplants
   eggplant and tomato
      chutney 108, *109*
   roasted eggplant and
      ricotta with walnuts and
      pomegranate *154,* 155
eggs
   bagel with pulled chicken,
      miso mayonnaise and
      garlic chips *28,* 29
   Cornersmith poached egg
      roll *66,* 67
   how to poach eggs 261
   leek, apple and goat's curd
      frittata 132, *133*
   poached egg, pomelo and
      hazelnuts with brussels
      slaw and whey dressing
      202, 203
escabeche of whiting 30, *31*

farro and zucchini salad with
   toasted hazelnuts 74, *75*
fennel
   citrus-braised fennel
      140, 141
   fennel flowers and honey
      with ricotta and figs on
      toast 78, *79*
   fennel, orange and chilli
      salt *32,* 33
   piccalilli *236,* 237
   pickled fennel with chilli
      220, *221*
   pork chops with fennel,
      apple sauce and mustard
      156, *157*
fermented fruit and vegetables
   fermented carrots 224, *225*

fermented pineapple and
   chilli sambal 114, *115*
   how to make 256, 259
fetta with roasted beetroot
   and rhubarb salad 213
figs
   figs and ricotta on toast
      with honey and fennel
      flowers 78, *79*
   tomato and fig salad *76,* 77
fish
   barbecued with grilled
      capsicum, herb salad
      and preserved lemon
      aioli *92,* 93
   escabeche of whiting 30, *31*
   pickled sardines *144,* 145
Franca's cheesecake *56,* 57
Franca's dark chocolate tart
   243, *244*
Franca's sugar plum buns
   183, *184*
frittata, leek, apple and goat's
   curd 132, *133*
fruit
   making chutneys and
      relishes 256
   making jam 250–252
funnels 248, 250

garlic chips, miso mayonnaise
   and pulled chicken bagel
   28, 29
gazpacho, cherry and tomato
   90, *91*
gingerbread layer cake with
   rhubarb, ricotta and
   walnuts 188, *189*
goat's curd, apple and leek
   frittata 132, *133*
grapes, pickled 164, *165,* 217
green beans
   green bean, baby cos and
      nashi pear salad with
      miso dressing 84, *85*
   piccalilli *236,* 237
green tomatoes *see* tomatoes
greens
   chard and wild greens pie
      204–205, *206*
   greens with pickled
      cumquats 42, *43*

ham, in poached egg roll
   66, 67
hazelnuts
   carrot loaf 192, *193*

267

hazelnut meringue cake with lime curd, peach and mango *120, 121*
hazelnuts, pomelo and poached egg with brussels slaw and whey dressing *202, 203*
toasted hazelnuts with farro and zucchini salad *74, 75*
toasting 261
heat-processing *254,* 255
herbs 260
hibiscus and rhubarb *58, 59*
honey and fennel flowers with ricotta and figs on toast *78, 79*
hot pink turnips *48, 49*

ice blocks, mulberry yoghurt *62,* 63

Jaimee's sauerkraut *148,* 149
'jam sugar' 251
jam triangles 199
jams
    blackberry *124, 125*
    carrot 200, *201*
    chilli 54, *55*
    making jam and marmalade 250–252
    mandarin and star anise *198,* 199
    peach and lime *72, 73*
    quince and apple *128, 129*
    strawberry, rhubarb and rose 14, *15*
jars, for preserving 250

kale, apple, sprouts and seed salad with buttermilk dressing *134,* 135
ketchup 107
kohlrabi, cabbage and spring herb slaw with pickled cumquats 42, *43*
Kristen's baked ricotta *232,* 233
Kristen's labneh *36, 37*
Kristen's ricotta cream 187

labneh *36, 37*
lacto-fermentation 259
lamb
    lamb tagine with prunes and fresh turmeric 228–229, *230*
    meatballs, broad beans and yoghurt 40, *41*
leek, apple and goat's curd frittata *132, 133*
lemons
    citrus-braised fennel *140,* 141
    lemon cordial 68, *69*
    lemon, pear and rosemary chutney *162,* 163
    preserved lemon aioli *96, 97*
    preserved lemon aioli and herb salad with barbecued fish and capsicum *92, 93*
    preserved lemon and white bean mash *222,* 223
    preserved lemons 214, *215*
lettuce, green bean and nashi pear salad with miso dressing *84, 85*
limes
    bitter lime marmalade *126,* 127
    carrot jam 200, *201*
    lime and peach jam *72, 73*
    lime curd, peach and mango with hazelnut meringue cake *120,* 121
    preserved limes 214

mackerel with grilled capsicum, herb salad and preserved lemon aioli *92, 93*
Maeve's baked apples 180, *181*
mandarin and star anise jam *198,* 199
mango, peach and lime curd with hazelnut meringue cake *120,* 121
marmalade
    bitter lime marmalade *126,* 127
    making marmalade 250–252
mascarpone, wattleseed, with persimmons *186,* 187
mayonnaise, garlic chips and pulled chicken bagel *28,* 29
meatballs, broad beans and yoghurt 40, *41*
meringue cake with lime curd, peach and mango *120,* 121
meringue sticks, cocoa and wattleseed 242, *244–245*
milkshakes, apricot and cardamom *118, 119*
miso
    bagel with pulled chicken, miso mayonnaise and garlic chips *28,* 29
    green bean, baby cos and nashi pear salad with miso dressing *84, 85*
muesli, toasted *16,* 17
mulberries
    mulberry compote 63
    mulberry yoghurt ice blocks *62,* 63
mushrooms
    dried mushrooms 171
    mushroom salt 171
    pine mushroom schnitzels *174,* 175
mustard
    Cornersmith mustard *158,* 159
    ploughman's plate 160, *161*
    pork chops with mustard, fennel and apple sauce 156, *157*

naan bread with red cabbage slaw, spiced pork and veal and green tomato relish *88,* 89
nasturtium butter and watercress with radishes *130,* 131
nuts, toasting 261

oats, in toasted muesli *16,* 17
oils 260
olive oil 260
oranges
    citrus-braised fennel *140,* 141
    orange and carrot soup *208,* 209
    orange, fennel and chilli salt *32,* 33

pans, for preserving 248
paprika and rosemary toasted almonds 34, *35*
parsley tabouleh with radicchio and pomegranate *138, 139*
passata 106
Patrice's tomato ketchup 107
peaches
    peach and lime jam *72, 73*
    peach, lime curd and mango with hazelnut

meringue cake 120, 121
pearled spelt and zucchini salad with toasted hazelnuts 74, 75
pears
   nashi pear, baby cos and green bean salad with miso dressing 84, 85
   pear, lemon and rosemary chutney 162, 163
   poached in red wine 240, 241, 244
peas
   spring green salad 18, 19
   vegetable and chicken soup 24–25, 26–27
pectin 250, 251
pepper 260
persimmons with wattleseed mascarpone 186, 187
piccalilli 236, 237
pickles
   bread and butter cucumbers 110, 111, 112–113
   chokos 226, 227
   cumquats 234, 235
   dilly beans 116, 117
   fennel with chilli 220, 221
   green chillies 44, 45
   heat-processing 254, 255
   how to make 252, 255–256
   piccalilli 236, 237
   radishes 46, 47
   red grapes 164, 165
   sardines 144, 145
   storing of 255
pie, chard and wild greens 204–205, 206
pine mushroom schnitzels 174, 175
pineapple and chilli sambal 114, 115
ploughman's plate 160, 161
poached egg roll 66, 67
pomegranates
   pomegranate and radicchio with bittersweet tabouleh 138, 139
   pomegranate and walnuts with ricotta and roasted eggplant 154, 155
   pomegranate syrup 142, 143
   spiced veal and pork with pomegranate syrup 86, 87
pomelo, hazelnuts and poached egg with brussels slaw and whey dressing 202, 203

pork
   pork chops with fennel, apple sauce and mustard 156, 157
   spiced pork and veal, red cabbage slaw and green tomato relish with naan bread 88, 89
   spiced pork and veal with pomegranate syrup 86, 87
potato salad 146, 147
preserving
   equipment 248, 250
   fermenting 256, 259
   making chutneys and relishes 256, 257
   making jam and marmalade 250–252
   pectin and acid in fruit 251
   pickling 252, 255–256
   sterilising jars and bottles 250
prunes and fresh turmeric with lamb tagine 228–229, 230
pulses, sprouting 261
pumpkin seeds 261
purple carrot loaf 192, 193

quick pickled radishes 46, 47
quince and apple jam 128, 129

radicchio and pomegranate with bittersweet tabouleh 138, 139
radishes
   with nasturtium butter and watercress 130, 131
   pickled radishes 46, 47
   ploughman's plate 160, 161
red grapes, pickled 164, 165, 217
relishes
   green tomato relish 50
   how to make 256, 257
Reuben-style sandwich 210, 211
rhubarb
   rhubarb and hibiscus 58, 59
   rhubarb, ricotta and walnuts with gingerbread layer cake 188, 189
   rhubarb, strawberry and rose jam 14, 15
   roasted rhubarb and beetroot salad with fetta 213

ricotta
   Franca's cheesecake 56, 57
   Kristen's baked ricotta 232, 233
   Kristen's ricotta cream 187
   ricotta and figs on toast with honey and fennel flowers 78, 79
   ricotta and green tomato salad 22, 23
   ricotta and roasted eggplant with walnuts and pomegranate 154, 155
   ricotta, rhubarb and walnuts with gingerbread layer cake 188, 189
rose, rhubarb and strawberry jam 14, 15
rosemary
   rosemary and smoky paprika toasted almonds 34, 35
   rosemary, lemon and pear chutney 162, 163

salads
   green bean, baby cos and nashi pear salad with miso dressing 84, 85
   green tomato and ricotta salad 22, 23
   herb salad and preserved lemon aioli with barbecued fish and grilled capsicum 92, 93
   kale, apple, sprouts and seed salad with buttermilk dressing 134, 135
   potato salad 146, 147
   roasted beetroot and rhubarb salad with fetta 213
   roasted spiced cauliflower salad 216, 217, 218
   spring green salad 18, 19
   tomato and fig salad 76, 77
   zucchini and farro salad with toasted hazelnuts 74, 75
salsa, corn 166, 167
salt
   fennel, orange and chilli 32, 33
   in lacto-fermentation 259
   mushroom salt 171
   in recipes 260
salting (pickling) 252

sambal, chilli and fermented
    pineapple 114, *115*
sandwich, Cornersmith
    Reuben-style 210, *211*
sardines, pickled 144, 145
sauces
    apple sauce with cider
        150, *151*
    green tomato hot sauce 51
    tomato 41
sauerkraut *148, 149,* 210
schnitzels, pine mushroom
    174, 175
seeds, toasting 261
setting point 250, 251
soups
    carrot and orange *208,* 209
    tomato and cherry
        gazpacho 90, *91*
    vegetable and chicken
        24–25, 26–27
spring green salad 18, *19*
sprouts
    how to sprout pulses 261
    sprouts, kale, apple and
        seed salad with buttermilk
        dressing *134,* 135
star anise and mandarin jam
    198, 199
Steph's gingerbread layer
    cake with rhubarb, ricotta
    and walnuts 188, *189*
strawberry, rhubarb and rose
    jam 14, *15*
sugar, in jam-making 250
sugar plum buns 183, *184*
sunflower seeds 261
syrups
    hibiscus and rhubarb
        58, *59*
    pomegranate syrup
        142, *143*

tabouleh with radicchio and
    pomegranate 138, *139*
tagine of lamb with prunes
    and fresh turmeric
    228–229, *230*
tart, dark chocolate 243, *244*
toasted hazelnuts with farro
    and zucchini salad 74, *75*
toasted muesli *16,* 17
Tomato Day 98, *98–103,* 101
tomatoes
    bottled tomatoes *104,* 105
    green tomato and ricotta
        salad *22,* 23
    green tomato hot sauce 51

green tomato relish 50
green tomato relish with
    spiced veal and pork, red
    cabbage slaw and naan
    bread *88,* 89
lamb tagine with prunes and
    fresh turmeric
    228–229, *230*
Patrice's tomato ketchup 107
tabouleh with radicchio and
    pomegranate 138, *139*
tomato and cherry
    gazpacho 90, *91*
tomato and eggplant
    chutney 108, *109*
tomato and fig
    salad *76,* 77
tomato passata 106
trading 194, 197
turmeric and prunes with
    lamb tagine 228–229, *230*
turnips, hot pink *48,* 49

vanilla custard 182
veal
    spiced veal and pork, red
        cabbage slaw and green
        tomato relish with naan
        bread *88,* 89
    spiced veal and pork with
        pomegranate syrup 86, *87*
vegetables
    how to pickle 252, 255–256
    making chutneys and
        relishes 256
    piccalilli *236,* 237
    vegetable and chicken
        soup *24–25, 26–27*
vinegar 252, 256, 260

walnuts
    carrot loaf 192, *193*
    toasting 261
    walnuts and pomegranate
        with ricotta and roasted
        eggplant *154,* 155
    walnuts, ricotta and
        rhubarb with gingerbread
        layer cake 188, *189*
water bathing 255
watercress and nasturtium
    butter with radishes
    130, 131
wattleseeds
    wattleseed and cocoa
        meringue sticks
        242, *244–245*

wattleseed mascarpone
    with persimmons *186,* 187
whey
    whey caramel 238, *239*
    whey dressing on brussels
        slaw with pomelo,
        hazelnuts and poached
        egg *202,* 203
white bean and preserved
    lemon mash *222,* 223
whiting
    escabeche of 30, *31*
    grilled, with grilled
        capsicum, herb salad
        and preserved lemon
        aioli *92,* 93
wine, pears poached in
    240, 241, 244

yoghurt
    mulberry yoghurt ice
        blocks *62,* 63
    yoghurt, meatballs and
        broad beans 40, *41*

zucchini and farro salad with
    toasted hazelnuts 74, *75*

ACKNOWLEDGEMENTS

Our ongoing commitment to seasonality means that this book has taken over a year to come together. Through spring, summer, autumn and winter, we have worked with a team of people who believed in our vision, despite how very long it took! There are so many people to thank after such a project, but we definitely could not have done this without the support of the Murdoch team. We especially thank Jane Morrow, for holding our hands through our first cookbook experience; Alan Benson, for his beautiful images; David Morgan, for making it all look so good; and Virginia Birch, Alison Cowan, Katy Holder and Hugh Ford, for their patience and expertise.

To the Cornersmith family, there are too many of you to name, but each of you has helped to create the cafe and picklery – we thank you all.

We are indebted to our wonderful chef Sabine Spindler. We adore you, and will always remember this experience.

Thank you also to Madeleine Dobbins, who made the picklery what it is – and for your recipe testing, your enthusiasm and hand-modelling!

Thank you to Franca Zingler, Stephanie Lui and Patrice Moonen, Mirra Whale, Shane Roberts and Amanda Roberts, for their recipes, knowledge and commitment to Cornersmith.

We are grateful to Tia Jones and Nat Batger, for keeping us organised and on track – there is never a dull moment working with you ladies. To our other wife, Sonia Tsai, there are no words. We love you.

There are some people we could never thank enough: Jaimee Edwards, Holly Throsby, Kristen Allan and Cameron Krone, for being there from the beginning. We feel like you have always got our back.

Thank you to our endlessly supportive families and our beautiful children, Maeve and Max.

And finally, to the community of Marrickville – our customers, traders and students – you inspire us daily.

Published in 2015 by Murdoch Books, an imprint of Allen & Unwin

Murdoch Books Australia
83 Alexander Street
Crows Nest NSW 2065
Phone: +61 (0) 2 8425 0100
Fax: +61 (0) 2 9906 2218
murdochbooks.com.au
info@murdochbooks.com.au

Murdoch Books UK
Erico House, 6th Floor
93–99 Upper Richmond Road
Putney, London SW15 2TG
Phone: +44 (0) 20 8785 5995
murdochbooks.co.uk
info@murdochbooks.co.uk

For Corporate Orders & Custom Publishing contact
Noel Hammond, National Business Development Manager,
Murdoch Books Australia

Publisher: Jane Morrow
Design: Hugh Ford
Editorial Manager: Virginia Birch
Editor: Alison Cowan
Food Editor: Katy Holder
Photographer: Alan Benson
Stylist: David Morgan
Production Manager: Mary Bjelobrk

Text © Alex Elliott-Howery and James Grant 2015
The moral rights of the authors have been asserted.
Design © Murdoch Books 2015
Photography © Alan Benson 2015

All rights reserved. No part of this publication may be reproduced, stored in a retrieval system or transmitted in any form or by any means, electronic, mechanical, photocopying, recording or otherwise, without the prior written permission of the publisher.

A cataloguing-in-publication entry is available from the catalogue of the National Library of Australia at nla.gov.au.

ISBN 978 1 74336 296 9 Australia
ISBN 978 1 74336 329 4 UK

A catalogue record for this book is available from the British Library.

Colour reproduction by Splitting Image Colour Studio Pty Ltd, Clayton, Victoria

Printed by 1010 Printing International Limited, China

IMPORTANT: Those who might be at risk from the effects of salmonella poisoning (the elderly, pregnant women, young children and those suffering from immune deficiency diseases) should consult their doctor with any concerns about eating raw eggs.

OVEN GUIDE: You may find cooking times vary depending on the oven you are using. For fan-forced ovens, as a general rule, set the oven temperature to 20°C (35°F) lower than indicated in the recipe.

MEASURES GUIDE: We have used 20 ml (4 teaspoon) tablespoon measures. If you are using a 15 ml (3 teaspoon) tablespoon add an extra teaspoon of the ingredient for each tablespoon specified.